THE CASE FOR A CREATOR

FOR KIDS

Other books in the Lee Strobel series for kids

The Case For Christ For Kids
The Case For Faith For Kids
Off My Case For Kids

The Case For A CREATOR
FOR KIDS

Lee Strobel with Rob Suggs

zonderkidz

WILLOW
Willow Creek Association

ZONDERVAN.COM/
AUTHORTRACKER

The children's group of Zondervan

www.zonderkidz.com

The Case for a Creator for Kids
Copyright © 2006 by Lee Strobel
Illustrations copyright © 2006 by The Zondervan Corporation

Requests for information should be addressed to:
Grand Rapids, Michigan 49530

Library of Congress Cataloging-in-Publication Data
Applied for

Editor: Kristen Tuinstra
Cover Design: Sarah Jongsma and Holli Leegwater
Interior Art Direction: Sarah Jongsma and Kristen Tuinstra
Interior design: Sarah Jongsma
Composition: Ruth Bandstra
Illustrations: Dan Brawner
Photography: Synergy Photographic

Printed in the United States of America

06 07 08 09 10 • 8 7 6 5 4 3 2 1

TABLE of CONTENTS

WHO YA GONNA BELIEVE?

There you are sitting in science class at school. You're thinking...

Say, what *are* you thinking? What are your feelings about science in general? Not as cool as a science-fiction movie? More fun than having a cavity drilled? Your true answer is in there somewhere.

Either way, it's science class. And it's an interesting one today, because Mr. Axiom, the science teacher, is starting a new unit on how the world began. You hear something about a Big Bang, and how all the stuff that made up the entire universe was gummed up into one puny little wad before it blew up. And how that stuff is *still* exploding outward, as it has since the beginning.

The story line could use a few aliens and starships, but all in all, it's really pretty cool. The Big Bang doesn't sound too scientific, but again—pretty cool!

> Science: what's observed in the way things happen.

Fast-forward a couple of days. Now you're in Sunday school. Mrs. Homily, the teacher, is starting a new unit on the first book of the Bible, called Genesis. She starts with the very first words of Genesis, "In the beginning God created the heavens and the earth."

The kids are kind of nodding along, but you have a big question about all this. Why aren't Mrs. Homily and Mr. Axiom on the same page? They seem to have two completely different stories for the same subject. Mr. Axiom says the universe came from a big explosion; Mrs. Homily claims it came from God. Who's right and who's wrong?

What really bothers you the most is that Mr. Axiom, the science guy, seems to make the best case for his claims. A humongous, long-ago explosion is a pretty wild story, to be honest, but he makes it believable. He gives numbers and details, and tells why the scientists came up with their ideas.

Evidence (EV-eh-dents): proof that something happened.

You've always liked Mrs. Homily. What's weird is that she's only telling you what your parents might have told you all your life: God made everything. You've always liked church and gone along with the program. But you're not a little kid anymore. You're going to be a teenager soon. You're beginning to think

things through for yourself. And you're noticing that neither Mrs. Homily nor anyone at church is too concerned
about ... well, the *reasons* and the *evidence* for what they're
teaching you. Not as much as in science class.

For example, you see a baseball lying in a pile of broken glass next to a window. That's your *evidence* that the
baseball broke the window. Better hope that baseball isn't
yours!

Q4U:

What do you like or dislike about science? What
kinds of science subjects have you enjoyed studying
most?

CASE NOTES

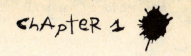

chAPteR 1

How Do You Fit ALL the Pieces Together?

So you've decided to assemble the whole puzzle for yourself—at least as many pieces as someone your age can handle. Who is right? Science or God? School or church? Both? Neither?

Beginning the search

Get ready to do some detective work. You'll look for clues about how the world got here and whether God had anything to do with it—or whether there is a God in the first place.

But that's not so easy, is it? Since God is supposed to be invisible, and since he would have put this world together a long time ago, how will you get to the truth of the matter?

Well, it's all about detective work. Imagine you're looking for answers about some other question. Pretend there's an elephant on your roof. One day you're leaving for school, and you see the massive fellow sitting there on top of your house. Whoever was in charge of this elephantine act is no longer on the scene. But your mom wants to know how that elephant got up there. (How to get him down would also be helpful information!) Where would you begin your investigation?

First, you might look for physical evidence. Are there footprints on the grass? A ramp or a ladder? Any cranes or elephant-moving equipment? You might take a walk all around the house and look closely for any changes. Whatever you find may tell you something about who might have put the elephant up there, and when it might have happened.

It might be a good idea to talk to some of the neighbors. Did they hear any strange noises? See any strange people? Maybe someone saw how the elephant was placed on the roof. It would also be a good idea to learn something about elephants. You might go to the zoo and talk to an elephant expert.

> Conclusion: an opinion decided based on facts. In the broken window example earlier, your conclusion is realizing the baseball broke the window.

In other words, you would gather information by doing three things: looking, thinking, and asking. Finally, you would put together everything you learned and come to the best conclusion possible. Even if you couldn't absolutely prove the *who* and the *how* of the elephant caper, you might get enough information to make a very good guess.

That's exactly how you would do your investigation of God. He himself may be invisible, but the evidence is not. You can look closely at several kinds of science. You can also talk to some really brainy scientists and experts who have already been collecting the clues.

You can look very carefully.

You can ask the best questions.

You can think about what you learn.

Then you can make the best decisions.

Any good scientist will tell you there is one important rule: follow the evidence wherever it leads you. For example, you might find trustworthy evidence that purple–polka–dotted aliens placed the elephant on the roof. That might be the best evidence you have. If so, your best guess would be that purple–polka–

dotted aliens put an elephant on your roof—even if it sounds ridiculous, and even if people would laugh! Good science is *objective*—that means it looks only at the evidence, even if the evidence points to something you don't want to believe.

> Being objective: to figure stuff out based on facts, not your own opinions.

What if you want to believe in God? Look at the evidence, then make up your mind.

What if you want to believe there is no God? Same deal.

Q4U:

Have you had to solve a mystery lately — such as a missing TV remote, for instance? How did you look, ask, think, and decide?

Three big questions

So what are the areas of science to think about? There are many to explore, but there are three important areas.

1. The first is called *cosmology*. That's the study of how the universe was formed. What can scientists tell you about the beginning of the world? And what can you conclude about whether God was involved or whether the universe came to be in some other way?

2. Next are *physics* and *astronomy*. Physics tells how things work in the world. For instance, if an elephant falls off your roof, it is because of gravity—and that's physics. If purple-polka-dotted aliens put the elephant there, they might have come from outer space—and that deals with astronomy.

Your body is made up of cells. Cells are teeny-tiny things (you can't see them without a microscope) made up of even tinier things called proteins. Imagine a snowflake. Millions and millions of snowflakes packed together make a snowman — just like millions and millions of cells make you.

3. Last is to take a look at DNA and the question of human life. DNA is basically the instruction manual for building proteins, which make up the cells of all living things—including you. Is there any evidence that an intelligent designer put this complicated information into DNA? If not, where does the evidence lead?

After you examine these three big questions, you'll be in a better position to decide what you think about the biggest question of all—whether there is a case for a creator. After that comes one final question: When the conclusion is made, what should you do about it? How should you live?

What you should do about it right now is turn the page!

CASE NOTES

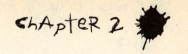

chApteR 2

DiD It ALL StARt WitH A BiG BANG?

Okay, you've got to admit that an elephant on the roof is not something you see every day. You would have to immediately ask the question: how did it even get there?

But believe it or not, you see something much more amazing every day—and probably hardly give it a second thought. You see, there's a wide, wild, wonderful world around you. It's filled with blue oceans and skies, snowcapped mountains, and green valleys. All kinds of plants grow, and millions of animals creep, crawl, swim, and fly across it. The world has penguins

Does seeing the world every day make you take it for granted? Does seeing it every day make it any less incredible?

and pandas, giraffes and gerbils, snakes and shrimp. And the planet spins in just the right way to give us and our animal friends bright days for doing our thing, and dark nights for sleeping.

It might be hard to get an elephant on your roof, but it would be tons more difficult to put all this stuff together and wrap it up in one planet—not to mention the galaxy and the universe where the world spins.

Sooner or later you have that thought: *Hey, this world is an amazing place, one blue-and-green marble out there among billions of miles of black space and barren rocks. How did this big marble get here?*

Cosmologist: a scientist who studies the beginning of the universe.

Theory: an explanation to answer a question.

There are scientists who spend all their time trying to figure out how the universe got started. *Cosmologists* are interested in that question. Just like a detective searching for clues to solve a mystery, you'll start by learning what *theories* or explanations the cosmologists have come up with.

Matter: anything that has form and takes up room; the stuff everything is made of. Matter is all of the cells that make up this book, dirt, carpeting, toys, and even your body. If someone needs to drop a few pounds, they should say they need to *lose matter* instead of *lose weight*!

That was a blast!

Most cosmologists believe it all started with a bang. And they mean exactly what they say.

Here's how it happened, in cosmologists' view:

All matter—every last bit of all the stuff that *every-thing* is made of—was clumped together very, very, very tightly into a very, very, very small space. Before, it was nothing at all! Suddenly, it all exploded with a mighty blast. Imagine pushing everything you own into your bedroom closet, then forcing the door shut with all your strength. You'd better get out of the way! Pretty soon all that stuff will fly through the air of your bedroom. Multiply that by several bajillions of gazillions, and you would have the Big Bang.

Photons: tiny particles of light.

Many scientists believe that when all those particles of matter exploded outward from the original wad of matter, they flew outward to fill the universe—and they're still moving, expanding the boundaries of the universe. Keep in mind that these particles were teeny tiny. The scientists call some of them *photons*—tiny particles that make light. So light filled the universe at the moment of this explosion came.

Tremendous Space Kablooie

In a famous cartoon strip, Calvin is a boy who talks to his imaginary tiger friend, Hobbes. Calvin wonders why something as amazing, mathematical, and scientific as the beginning of the universe would have a silly name like the Big Bang. Hobbes the tiger asks, "What would you call the creation of the universe?"

Calvin thinks for a moment and answers, "The Tremendous Space Kablooie!"

Many scientists began to use that name for the Big Bang, abbreviating it to the TSK!

The Big Bang, then, involved a great explosion of light. Hmmm. That seems familiar. It sounds just a bit like the first few sentences of the Bible, which say that in the beginning everything was "formless and empty" (NIV) and then God said, "Let there be light."

Scientists have spent years trying to understand the Big Bang. They attempt to guess what happened then by studying what is happening now.

Some of the scientists' ideas

Idea #1: Pop start!

The first idea scientists offer is that sometimes matter "just shows up" for no reason. Some scientists say

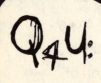

Read the first four verses of the book of Genesis from the Bible. How would you compare these events to the Big Bang account of the beginning of the universe?

that the universe could have started this way. This idea says there would be no creator and no particular reason—it just happened because it could. Presto! Instant universe.

But that doesn't seem very scientific. Remember, science is what is observed in the way things happen. You know an elephant couldn't just appear out of nowhere on your roof. Someone or something had to put it there.

Kalam Argument:

Everything that has a beginning has a cause.

The universe has a beginning.

So the universe has a cause.

Idea #2: A universe that was caused

Our second idea is based on some thinking by a Muslim who lived many centuries ago. It's called the Kalam Argument. Kalam is pronounced KA-lahm (no, not KA-blooie!). Here's how it works:

Read on to learn more about this argument. What are you waiting for, an argument?

CHAPTER 3

CAN YOU PUT KALAM to the Test?

Remember, the Kalam Argument is:

1. Everything that has a beginning has a cause.

2. The universe has a beginning.

3. So the universe has a cause.

1. Everything that has a beginning has a cause

The Kalam Argument says that nothing new is created without being *caused*.

Try it at home! Your mom says something like, "Who made these muddy footprints on the carpet?" You shrug and say you don't know. Your brothers and sisters just look at one another innocently. What does your mother say? "Well, they didn't get there by themselves!"

The next time she says that, congratulate her for applying the Kalam Argument. Everything that has a beginning has a cause. The footprints began to exist at a point in time—so they *must* have had a cause!

> Vacuum: completely empty space. It's not like the vacuum that sucks up dirt and dust at home. Say you attach a vacuum pump to a jar opening and suck out all the air so that nothing is left inside. Then seal the container before any air can get back in. What you'd have left inside is a vacuum — the kind you would find if you went to outer space. There's no air.

This point makes sense. But a few scientists are stubborn about their "pop start" theory. They speculate that the particles that make up the universe could have just popped out of nowhere from a certain kind of vacuum. A vacuum is usually defined as totally empty space. So who's right?

Energy: the ability to do work.

A professor named William Lane Craig has thought about this one for a long time. The vacuum that those scientists are talking about, he says, is not exactly "a big bunch of nothing" the way you imagined in the jar. This vacuum is full of energy. The vacuum and the energy locked up in the vacuum would have been the cause of those particles appearing—if that's what happened.

So that raises a very important question: who or what would have created this energy in the first place? Certainly its existence needs an explanation—and suddenly you're right back to the beginning of how the world got here! After all, this energy would seem to have needed a creator.

One thing seems like common sense: as far as human experience goes, nothing simply pops into existence on its own, out of nothing (the elephant can't appear out of nowhere). So the first step of the Kalam Argument holds up.

2. The universe has a beginning

When most scientists study all the facts and figures — and this can get pretty complicated — they become convinced that the universe had a beginning. And if there was truly a beginning, then there truly must be a cause. Just as the elephant on your

roof didn't just pop into existence, the universe didn't create itself! There must be something — or someone — who caused the Big Bang to go kablooie!

Here is how the Bible explains where it started: "In the beginning God created the heavens and the earth." For thousands of years the Bible and its readers have insisted that there was a first moment when the universe came into existence. But only in the last hundred years or so have scientists discovered that all the clues really do point toward the universe having a beginning.

What about the proof? There are two kinds of evidence that the universe had a beginning: mathematical points and scientific points.

Doing the math. Imagine you're going to a new movie on opening day. The line for tickets wraps around the edge of the mall and goes out of sight! If it's *infinite*, there would have to be people standing in that line as far back as you could check. In fact, there would be no beginning at all, just trillions upon trillions of people trying to get into the same movie theater. And they're in trouble, because there's only so much popcorn.

> Infinity (in-FIN-eh-tee): no limits; an end-less supply.

Of course, there couldn't be an endless line of people. In the same way, the universe couldn't just stretch into the past forever, because the events could not go further and further into the past *forever*. By the way, another word for *forever* is *infinity*—an endless supply. The problem is that it's hard to talk about infinity because everything you can see and touch has limits.

Here's another example of the absurdity of an infinite number of things. Let's say you had an infinite number of baseball cards and you gave ten million of them to your friend. You'd still have as many cards as you did before you gave those away! Crazy, huh? Well, the idea that the universe is infinitely old is just as nonsensical.

Doing the science. The math people show us the numbers. The scientists show us the clues. And the clues from science, including measurements that researchers have done with high-tech instruments, point to the universe beginning with a bang. As a matter of fact, nearly all of today's scientists believe in the great explosion of light at the first moment of this universe's life.

So to review the first two Kalam points, everything that has a beginning has a cause, and the universe has a beginning. All you have to do is add up those two points to discover…

3. The universe has a cause

Just as you would expect, something as big as the universe had to start somewhere. Think about it: you hear a "bang" from your bedroom, and your sister asks, "What was that?"

You reply from the living room, "Nothing." (Actually, you don't want her to know it's the stray elephant you sneaked into your bedroom, hoping to keep him for a pet.)

But your sister says, "That bang had to come from something." And of course, she's reminding you of the third part of the Kalam Argument. Now here's something to ponder: if a *little* bang had to have a cause, what about one as big as—well, everything all together?

What kind of cause could have started the entire universe? It must have been powerful, right? It must have been smart too, in order to make the explosion work just right. It must have been creative to come up with such a cool idea! It must have been timeless, because time wasn't even created until the Big Bang happened. It must have been immaterial, or without a physical body. In other words, like a spirit.

Hmmm. Sound familiar? That's a pretty good start to describing God.

Logic (LAH-jeck): it's kind of like common sense. Or to put it another way, logic is the study of the rules of reasoning. To have good arguments, you must obey the rules of logic or your argument isn't valid. The Kalam Argument obeys the rules of logic. If it's true that everything that begins to exist has a cause, and if it's true that the universe began to exist, then the rules of logic require the conclusion that the universe has a cause. That's logical, don't you think?

Could it be that Mr. Axiom, your science teacher, and Mrs. Homily, your Sunday school teacher, are *both* right? Details may differ, but they each agree that the universe was suddenly born in a flash of light at some point in the past. And logic tells you that the best explanation for all of this is a cause that looks suspiciously like the God of the Bible.

Wanted: dead or alive

Okay. So from the clues you read about, the universe points to a beginning. And it points to a *someone* who had to be there to start things up. But couldn't

he have "left the building"? All you can say is that at some point, there *was* a God. Science and mathematics point there, but no further. Right?

Not exactly. Consider these points:

- If someone is strong enough to create this whole universe, wouldn't he have to be strong enough to remain alive? Since he made the laws of nature, how could anything in them cause his death?

But who made God?

But doesn't God also need to have a cause?

No. Remember what you learned before — that *everything with a beginning* has to have a cause. Christians believe that God is eternal — he had no beginning and will have no end. In fact, before God created the universe, time didn't even exist. There was just timelessness.

Remember: since God didn't have a beginning, he didn't need a cause.

- You'll read later in the book how there is actually evidence that God is alive and well and still at work in his creation.

- Many scientists, like other people, say they get their clues about the Creator by knowing him as a friend. They point to many things that happen in their lives, and in the world, that show a creator is alive and well.

You still have a lot to read about! For one thing, it's time to take a look at physics and astronomy. Get on it!

Q4 4:

What do you think is the most sensible way to explain how the universe began? Why?

chApteR 4

DiD You Hit the cosmic LotteRY?

Place: outer space.

You are an astronaut on the first flight to Venus.

Pretty cool, huh? Your hyper–powered ship plunges through space at warp speed, boldly hanging out where no kid has hung out before. You begin to get excited as your landing craft touches down on a dusty plain on Venus. You get into your space suit, climb down the ladder, and there it is: an attractively painted sign that reads, "Welcome to the Venus Holiday Inn Express."

Then you look past the sign and notice the escalator. It's a moving stairway that descends into an opening in the ground, just like at the mall. As you step aboard, it carries you to a nice underground complex made of swanky rooms—a restaurant with the aroma of burgers and pizzas coming from its kitchen, a bedroom to rest in after your trip, a rec room with exercise equipment, an indoor pool, and other nice stuff. It's just like a fine hotel back on earth. The only thing missing is—um, other beings, whether earthly types or otherwise. But who cares? It's rockin'!

The first thing to do is take a shower and wash off all that space grunge. Then, on the powerful radioset next to your bed, you beam a message to earth. What to say? How about this?

Greetings from Venus, fellow earth-heads! Arrived safely. Found interesting natural formations on the planet, probably formed by random weather conditions over millions of years. Lucky for me, the random rock and land formations grew into a natural hotel complex complete with working electricity, food, comfy furniture, and HBO. Hey, what were the odds?

What were the odds? Do you think random weather conditions would create a working escalator, an interplanetary radio, exercise equipment, and even a greeting sign? The odds of all that happening *by accident* would be one to some number far too large to even print out in a book this size (and that wouldn't be a very exciting book anyway).

> What are *odds*? No, they're not a bunch of odd people. When someone asks, "What are the odds?" they're asking how likely it would be for something to happen. Say you buy one lottery ticket. And there's only one winning ticket out of a million tickets that were sold. Then your odds of buying that winning ticket would be one in a million. That's a long shot, don't you think?

So assuming you're halfway bright, you probably wouldn't send that message about "random weather conditions," would you? Of course not. More likely you would conclude that *someone had intentionally planned and built the interplanetary hotel complex.* Even though there's nobody around who might have done the job, that's still the most likely explanation.

Sure, it's a crazy story. But many scientists today would tell you that a swanky hotel on Venus—unplanned—is a lot like the idea of a complex universe without a builder.

Coincidences?

Robin Collins is pretty smart. He went to college and got degrees in physics, mathematics, and philosophy. Sometimes people feel sort of dumb around him, but luckily he doesn't make a big deal out of how smart he is.

He says that in the past thirty years, scientists have learned a lot of new things about the universe and how it's all arranged. They have noticed that wherever they look, things are set up in *exactly, precisely* the right way for life to exist. In every direction, some *huge* coincidence would be needed for the conditions to have just the right settings. And you would need a long string of these coincidences to occur *together*, side by side, at the same time, for life to be possible at all.

Many scientists agree with Dr. Collins. They make the point that the universe is exactly "fine-tuned" in such a way that it will support life. This is called the *anthropic principle*. That word *anthropic* comes from the Greek word for humanity. Think of one of those

circus acrobats walking across a tightrope. She has fine-tuned her sense of balance to such an amazing degree that she can walk several hundred feet without tipping over to the right or to the left. The universe is like that, according to these scientists. Against far more amazing odds, it has found a precise balance in all its physical conditions, in just such a way that you can live in it.

> Anthropic principle (an-THRAH-peck PRIN-suh-pull): the idea that the universe was created in exactly the right way to let human beings survive.

But has it "arranged itself," or has some being of higher intelligence done the arranging? That is the great question, isn't it? That underground hotel back on Venus seems far more likely to have been arranged by a "someone" than by random environmental conditions. And in the case of the tightrope, a baby couldn't crawl across the wire. It took a special athlete working very hard to *purposely* fine-tune the right balance.

Q4U:

What is one coincidence you have seen happen? How likely or unlikely was it?

In the same way, many scientists find it highly unlikely that random conditions in the universe would
fall into line in just such a way that people would have
a nice home—unless someone intentionally fine-
tuned the right balance.

Gravity: the tale of the tape

There's a bumper sticker that reads, "Gravity: It's not
just a good idea—it's the LAW!"

The law of gravity is an example of a kind of physics
you can easily understand. The earth pulls at everything that is either on it or close to it. It pulls at you,
and that's why you don't float off into the sky. It pulls
at the moon, and that's why the moon follows the
earth everywhere. The moon doesn't just figure it's a
good idea to follow the earth; it's the *law*.

> Law of gravity: attraction between two ob-
> jects. If you were to jump out of an airplane,
> you would eventually hit the ground (hope-
> fully you have a parachute!). The earth's
> gravity pulls you closer to it.

Gravity has a certain amount of strength. It could have been much weaker or much stronger, but it's set at a certain level. In fact, imagine a tape measure that stretches all the way across the universe—billions and billions of miles. Pretend it has marks at every inch. This represents the range along which gravity could have been set. However, it's set at one precise mark along that long tape measure—and because it's exactly where it needs to be, life is possible.

Now imagine the setting is changed by moving it just *one inch* on the tape measure. That's one inch compared to the width of the entire universe. Doesn't seem like much of an adjustment, does it? Actually, that small change could create a universe-wide catastrophe. Life would be destroyed everywhere. But because gravity is fixed at precisely the right location, life is possible. (Good thing, right?)

> If you could land on Jupiter and walk out of your spaceship, you'd practically be as flat as a pancake against the ground because the level of gravity is so strong.

Could that be just a coincidence? Something that worked out just on its own?

It's like hitting the cosmic lottery, isn't it? As you read earlier, when somebody wins the lottery, his or her chances may have been a million to one. But the chances of the universe having worked out just right on its own are much, much smaller—again, one chance in a number with so many zeros behind it you could not even print them out in this book.

A room full of monkeys

If gravity were the only condition required for life, you would be impressed at how perfectly the universe sets it up. But there are many other factors involved in making it possible for you to live, breathe, and exist. There are at least thirty separate necessities for living, and each one of them is finely tuned to allow you to exist.

There is an old saying that claims if you had a room full of monkeys and gave each one a computer with a keyboard, sooner or later one of them would produce a duplicate of one of Shakespeare's plays, like *Romeo and Juliet*. (Wouldn't you hate the job of checking their work?) It's not that one of the monkeys would become a great creative writer—just that he would hit all the right keys by chance. The question is, how many bajillions of years would it take for that to happen?

A scientist speaks

"A commonsense and satisfying interpretation of our world suggests the designing hand of a super-intelligence." — Owen Gingerich, Harvard astronomy professor and senior astronomer at the Smithsonian Astrophysical Observatory

The universe is like that, only it's much more complicated than a single play by Shakespeare. The earth is an orderly place that allows a variety of life-forms—a possibility that is so, so, so fragile. Is it easier to explain by coincidence, like monkeys tapping away at the keyboard? Or is it easier to explain as a personal, intentional work of superintelligence and creativity? The theory of *intelligent design* covers the second choice.

> Some necessities for living are food, water, and air. Gravity is one of them. Without gravity, you would float to outer space. By the way, so would your food, water, and air!

Another example of "fine-tuning" is the *cosmological constant*. Pretty fancy name, huh? So what does it mean? It's the energy density of empty space. So what does *that* mean?

As you look at all the factors making life possible in the universe, do you believe it's likely that there are other planets with life? Why or why not?

Well, here's what you need to know about the cosmological constant: it had to be set absolutely perfectly, or a terrible disaster would have resulted. If it had been adjusted just slightly in one direction, stars and planets could never have formed. If it had been changed just slightly in the other direction, the whole universe would have collapsed upon itself. Instead, the cosmological constant is one exact mark on the tape measure—the only mark that will allow life to exist in the universe.

How precise is the cosmological constant? "Let's say you were way out in space and were going to throw a dart at random toward the earth," Dr. Robin Collins said. "It would be like successfully hitting a bull's-eye that's one-trillionth of a trillionth of an inch in diameter. That's less than the size of one solitary atom."

Intelligent Design (in-TELL-eh-jent dee-ZINE): the belief that the order of the universe and its living things shows evidence of a thinking designer rather than coincidence.

Now, take the two measurements you've learned: gravity and the cosmological constant. Getting the precise setting of either one alone is more amazing than you can imagine. But the two *together*? According to Dr. Collins, the chances of that are about one part in a hundred million trillion trillion trillion trillion trillion trillion. Try counting to that number sometime when you can't sleep!

Now consider that there are many other measurements found in physics. Imagine a giant dashboard, like the one in a car, with all those readings. You can believe either that they have set themselves on their own, or that someone has sat in the driver's seat and carefully set them at the right readings. Intelligent design says there must be a driver.

Designing minds

Dr. Collins makes an interesting point. He says that the more he studies the universe, the more amazed he is.

"Only recently have we discovered how precise every condition had to be, in so many areas, for us to have this universe that allows life," he said. "The deeper we dig, we see that God is more subtle and more ingenious and more creative than we ever thought possible.

And I think that's the way God created the universe for us—to be full of surprises."

So what's your take? Did you start with a big bang and end up—just by chance—with thinking people who live in a wonderful world of grassy fields, oceans, blue skies, and four seasons? If so, people won the lottery of all lotteries. There could have been a massive universe made up only of flying rocks, and created by no one in particular for no purpose in particular.

But look around you! It's not too hard to agree with more and more scientists who look away from their telescopes and microscopes and say, "Somebody up there likes us!"

And you haven't even read about DNA yet!

chapter 5

Could God Be the Intelligent Designer?

There's a board game called Mousetrap. It's all about building a "machine" that is much more complicated than it needs to be—and much more fun! There's a bathtub on top of a pole, a little man who launches off a springboard, a little silver ball that rolls down a chute, a stick with a boot at the end that kicks the ball down that chute when something nudges it, and lots of other junkyard treasures. In the game, you assemble the trap by adding each crazy piece.

It may be the most enjoyable mousetrap you can build, but it certainly isn't the simplest. You can find the simpler kind at your local hardware store—or at the office of Michael Behe, a respected biochemist. He is the type of scientist who studies what living things are made of, especially what the chemicals are up to inside them. And he loves playing with one of those simple mousetraps made of a rectangle of wood. You have to worry about his fingers. But he shows you

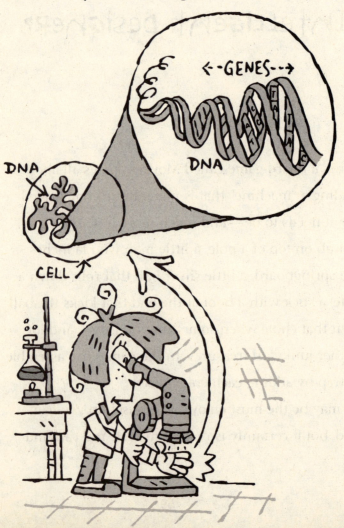

each of the parts—the base, the catch, the spring, the holding bar, and the hammer—and how they work together.

Then you go, "Wait a minute! I thought you were into chemicals and cells and stuff."

And he goes, "I am. Now—which of these parts can I take away from the mousetrap and keep it working?"

And you go, "I don't know. Looks like you need 'em all."

And he goes, "Right!"

And you go, "So? Watch your fingers!"

And he goes, "So the mousetrap is an example of *irreducible complexity*. That means it is a machine that cannot be simplified any further and still do its job. Take away the hammer here, for instance, and how many mice could you still catch? One-third? One-half?"

"None? Hey! Watch your ..."

"Right again!" Then he stuffs the mousetrap back into a drawer. You sigh in relief.

He goes, "The cell is run by irreducibly complex micromachines."

That's right—there are microscopic motors and systems in living organisms—including you! In a way, they're like the mousetrap because a certain number of their parts must be in place for the machine or system to work.

Irreducible complexity (EAR-reh-doo-seh-bull cuhm-PLEHCKS-eh-dee): the simplest possible arrangement of a machine for doing a job.

For example, some bacteria have a teeny, tiny motor and a rotary propeller to help them move through liquids—a motor so advanced that it spins faster than the engine on those fancy sports cars you see on the covers of car magazines. A professor at Harvard University says it's the most efficient motor in the universe, but it's so small your eye can't even see it—no matter how hard you squint!

Here's the point: It's impossible for the parts of this microscopic motor to have suddenly come together on their own, and there's no known way they could have been pieced together by themselves over time. So that leaves one other explanation: that there's a designer behind them.

"If the creation of a simple device like a mousetrap requires Intelligent Design," said Dr. Behe, "then we have to ask, 'What about the finely tuned machines of the cellular world?'"

If there's no natural way these machines could have been built on their own, he said, then other explanations should be considered.

After years of research and study, Dr. Behe has reached his own conclusion. "I believe," he said, "that irreducibly complex systems are strong evidence of a purposeful, intentional design by an intelligent agent. No other theory succeeds."

Could that "intelligent agent" be the same one who wrote the assembly instructions for all the parts of your body? Wait a minute! Who said anything about assembly instructions?

Biochemistry (BY-oh-kem-ess-tree): the study of stuff found in living things, and of the chemical activities that take place in living things.

Assembly instructions and biology

Have you ever put together something that's pretty complicated, like a model airplane that started out as a box full of seemingly unrelated pieces? What guided you to put the right parts together—this little widget attaching to this gizmo, this tab inserting into that slot? That's right—grab the instructions! Without them, the chances of building an airplane on your own would be really slim.

Now think about a *real* airplane, like a giant airliner that carries hundreds of people. Millions of parts have to be fit together in precisely the right way in order to build an airplane that seems to defy gravity as it soars through the sky. Without assembly instructions, it would be impossible to guess how to put together a safe and working airplane.

Think about this: you are much more complex than any airplane. Human beings can build airplanes, but they can't build a human being like you. How did the trillions of cells that make up your body get put together exactly so? Right again—assembly instructions!

Your body is composed of one hundred trillion microscopic cells. If you were to crack open any one of those cells, you'd find a long, threadlike material coiled up inside. Stretch it out, and it would measure six feet long! On that thread would actually be a chemical alphabet containing the exact assembly instructions for all of the proteins to make your skin, organs, hands, eyes, and brain. It's kind of like a super–duper complex recipe!

> DNA: the "instruction manual" for building each life-form.

These assembly instructions are called DNA, which stands for DeoxyriboNucleic Acid. Long, threadlike structures known as chromosomes carry genes with their DNA information. These genes are passed on

BACTERIA

from parent to child. If you share your mother's blue eyes or your father's running speed, it is because the right genes were passed to you from that parent.

After many years of work, scientists finally mapped out the *billions* of codes that make up the entire set of human chromosomes. It was like the complete assembly instructions for putting together people like you. But who could have devised those billions of codes in the first place?

No, your parents didn't pass their blue jeans down to you. Have you ever noticed that sometimes kids might laugh exactly like one of their parents? Or be really good at a hobby like basketball, just like one of their parents? That's because kids received the same genes from the parent.

Scrambled letter game

Now it's time to think about spelling. Have you ever noticed how one misplaced letter can change the whole meaning of a word, then a sentence? You might tell someone, "I caught your act." But if you reversed two letters, you could have, "I caught your cat." There are twenty-six letters in the alphabet, and they can be scrambled and re-scrambled to make any word in the language. Language is like a careful game of Scrabble.

Think of DNA as an alphabet that conveys information. Instead of twenty-six letters, DNA has only four

letters that represent chemicals. Scientists use the letters *A, C, G,* and *T.* These letters spell out the exact way your body can put together the complicated proteins that make up your body. In fact, your body has thousands of different kinds of proteins that create your fingers and toes, teeth and eyes, ears and brain, and all of the organs, tissues, blood, and nerves inside you.

Bill Gates, president of Microsoft, has said that DNA is like a software program, but far more complex than any software program that has ever been written. Your computer is useful for homework, email, surfing the Internet, and playing computer games. But many, many software experts have labored for years to produce the codes that make that possible.

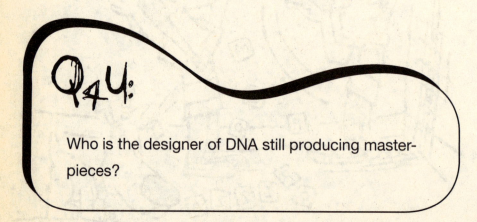

Q4U:

Who is the designer of DNA still producing masterpieces?

Do you think the far more complicated codes that provide the assembly instructions for every single person on earth—and every single human being who has ever lived—could be "written" without there being a software engineer of life?

Imagine opening a box of Scrabble tiles, shaking it up really good, and throwing all the tiles into the air. How would they land? If you were extremely fortunate, you might find that three or four letters have landed in such a way as to make a short word. The rest would be gibberish. But can you imagine throwing the letters into the air time after time and having them land in such a way that sentences, paragraphs, and whole books landed in order right in front of you? Seems awfully unlikely—unless some invisible intelligence had control over how those letters landed.

To sum it up: You live in the age of information. Think of all the information

1. on websites,

2. in emails,

3. that bounces off satellites and makes a cable television program in your living room,

4. in all the books in all the libraries in the world.

Every bit of *that* information is put together by human beings. You can't receive an email that wasn't written by a human being, see a television show that wasn't created by people, or read a book that had no human author.

Scientists discover more and more that life itself is made up of *information*, like the assembly instructions of DNA. That information is far more complicated and meaningful and exact than all the books and emails and television broadcasts in the world. Could it all come together to form the human population of earth just by "letter tiles" falling on a great biological playing board?

Wherever you see information of any kind, there was an intelligence behind it. Since there's information coded inside the DNA of every living person and thing, doesn't that mean life has an author? A designer with an intelligence far too great for anyone to understand?

Many scientists today believe that every cell in your body bears the signature of that designer in the DNA that's found there — and that he is very much alive, very well, and still producing masterpieces every day.

CASE NOTES

Chapter 6

Is This Your Final Answer?

At the beginning of this book, you learned about true science: following the facts no matter where they lead.

It's like putting together a big jigsaw puzzle, isn't it? In the beginning you have a great number of pieces with many combinations of colors and pieces of pictures. None of them alone tell the story. But as you put the puzzle together, a greater picture begins to assemble before your eyes. Your only job is to keep finding where the pieces go. When they're all in place, the picture is very clear.

How do you feel about the puzzle you put together in this book? Each chapter is a piece of the puzzle.

- Cosmology is the study of the origin of the universe. Everything that has a beginning has a cause behind it. Most scientists now believe the universe had a beginning at some point in the past. That means there must be a cause behind it—a powerful, smart, creative, timeless, and immaterial cause, like a spirit. In fact, like God.

- Physics is the study of energy and motion, and astronomy is the study of outer space. The conditions that make life possible in the universe are so specific, and so completely necessary, that it's hard to imagine anything more unlikely than for them to fall into place on their own. For example, if there was a teeny-tiny bit more gravity strength or a teeny-tiny bit less, the effect on life would be a disaster. Hmmm. Sounds like whoever created the universe must have really cared about people because he was so careful to create a safe and livable place for them.

- DNA contains the instructions for creating the human body, and biochemistry is the study of chemical activities that take place in living things. Your entire body is a fantastic complex – a whole world, really — of factories filled with micromachines that churn out all the work that makes it possible for you to eat, breathe, and do everything else. Living things contain microscopic machines that can't be explained by saying they somehow put themselves together. A more reasonable explanation is that there's a creator behind them. In fact, the assembly instructions for all living things are made up of information found in DNA. And wherever information is — whether in a book or a computer code — there's intelligence behind it. In the case of DNA, it's a superintelligence — something like God.

You may be thinking, *What to decide?*

What the scientists think

Some scientists decide there's no creator. They look at the universe and conclude it must have somehow been created without any help. They look at the vast complexity of living things and conclude that it's all a matter of cells that combined together over time through chance, until they somehow found their way toward becoming more complex life-forms. They believe God isn't needed in any of this, so he must be an idea made up by people.

Other scientists decide that there *must* be a creator. They say the universe and living things show too much order to believe otherwise. The combination of all the cells and all the chemicals and all the laws of physics would call for coincidences beyond any mathematical calculation—just to allow people to live. They look at the beauty of the earth, set in a cold and empty space. The four seasons. Wind and rain and everything you need—not only to live but also to enjoy life. They look at all these things and wonder how anyone could think that there is no intelligent being behind it all.

A brilliant surgeon named Viggo Olsen once believed there was no God. His wife shared his lack of belief. But the two of them finally decided to search out all the evidence, as you have started to do by reading this book. They were going to show once and for all how science disproved God. They began by attempting to list all the scientific errors in the Bible.

To their great shock, they couldn't find those mis-takes. When they checked out each supposed "error," they found out it wasn't a mistake after all. They had simply not understood what the Bible actually said.

As they looked at each area of science, they failed again and again to disprove God. Instead, they kept finding huge reasons to believe in God after all. Not only that, but they came to believe that science pointed to several specific truths about God:

- The universe was created, and it's packed with power—heat and energy, for instance. Therefore, it was created by a *mighty force*.
- They looked at the order in the universe and in the cell structure of human bodies, and decided that this creator must be *intelligent*.
- They looked at the ability of people to love and to have compassion, and concluded that people must have been created by someone with those same qualities.

Their conclusion was that there is a God who is very powerful, very intelligent, and very caring. And after they investigated history, as you can do if you read *The Case for Christ for Kids*, they were finally led to believe that Jesus Christ is God's Son, sent into this world to personally befriend the very people God created.

The Olsens set out to show there was no God, and particularly that Christianity was a myth. Instead, they found themselves wanting to know Jesus. They asked him to send them to the place where they could serve him best of all. They ended up in the suffering nation of Bangladesh, where they spent thirty-three years, worked to start 120 churches, and helped provide doctors and medicine for countless hungry and sick men, women, and children. They said this was the most wonderful and exciting and fulfilling adventure of their lives.

After working with Jesus among the poor, they were more convinced than ever that God is powerful, intelligent, and very loving.

Facts and faith

Like other scientists, the Olsens discovered that the greatest evidence of God is very personal. As interesting and informative as all the fields of science may be, their own experience was the final and most powerful item of evidence.

Many scientists believe in God not only because of what they see in microscopes and telescopes, but what they experience in *relationships*. They feel that God isn't just some cosmic force out there on the other side of their calculations and chemicals. They feel that he is someone right here living in their daily lives. In other words, faith begins where facts leave off.

So as the investigation comes to a close, it's time to decide what to do about it.

What do you think about God? Do you believe science points in his direction? If so, what do you think he is like?

And if you believe there is a God, what difference does that make in your life? Should you just say, "Oh, that's interesting!" and go on the way you were? Or should you live in a new way?

Would you agree that if there is a God, he went through a lot of trouble to leave all kinds of clues to his existence in cosmology, astronomy, physics, bio-chemistry, and DNA? Why would he do that? Because he wants you to find him!

And would you agree that if he is very mighty and very caring, as the Olsens decided, that he might be a wonderful friend for you?

If so, what's your final answer? That is, how do you respond to what you have decided?

People all over the world have found faith to match their facts. They love God, they enjoy his friendship, and they find great happiness in serving him every day.

> If you're interested in that kind of life, you might try an experiment. Try that faith out. Ask God to speak to your heart. Ask him to come into your life, just as a good friend would come into your home. See what happens. And as part of your experiment, talk to your parents about God.

Also, try doing something that you think God would want you to do, just as the Olsens did. You don't have to go to another country. Just try doing something nice for another person—someone in your family or at school. This is an important part of your experiment because God–believers say that doing what God likes helps you know God better.

As you grow each day, becoming older and smarter, keep experimenting! Continue to know God more and more. It's the greatest science project of all.

Off My CASE

FOR KIDS

12 STORIES TO HELP **YOU** DEFEND YOUR FAITH

Lee STROBEL AND Robert ELMER

zonder**kidz**

CHApTER 1

LyDiA, KiD MissioNARY

Lydia saw it coming, but that didn't make it hurt any less. She stepped high over Mandy Witherspoon's outstretched foot so she wouldn't trip, but she lost her grip on her books. And the kids' giggles made her face flush like fire.

"Come on, let's go!" The bus driver looked up in the rearview mirror and yelled at her. "And if you're late again tomorrow morning, you're going to have to walk."

Lydia held the tears in—just barely—scooped up her books, and scrambled off the bus as fast as her legs would take her.

"Speak English much?"

She didn't turn to see who had yelled the insult, but she could guess. Mandy Witherspoon. What did that girl have against her? She wished she didn't hear some of the taunts at school, wished she understood why some of the kids looked at her with so much hatred sometimes.

You don't belong here!

Get back over the border where you came from!

But we're not going back. Lydia stood in her muddy front yard for a minute, catching her breath and letting the rain wash the tears from her face. She didn't really miss what they'd left behind in Mexico. Except back there, everybody else was just as poor as Lydia and her grandmother. Just as poor, and just as desperate to find something better. At least here…

"At least here what, Lord?" she prayed out loud as she pushed open the front door to their apartment. Her thirteen-year-old sister wasn't home, as usual. And her grandmother would not return home for another two hours, maybe later, depending on what shift they gave her at the burger place. "What do we have now that's better than back home?"

Well, plenty, when she stopped to think about it. She sat down at the wobbly kitchen table and spread out her soggy books. Books, for one thing. A school to go to, and not all the kids were as mean as Mandy Witherspoon. A tiny apartment with a bathroom and a telephone. Three small rooms, which was not much compared to what a lot of other Americans had.

But compared to what they had back in Mexico? She would not soon forget the tar-paper shack they used to live in, her and a dozen other relatives: aunts and uncles and nieces and nephews, and all without a bathroom. She rested her head on her open English textbook for a minute, telling the Lord she was sorry for the way she complained. He had brought them here for a reason, she knew. She and Grandmother had prayed about it, looked for the answer.

"I'm sorry, God. Help me to know why I'm here, and what you want me to do."

But she was tired of trying to figure it out. Right now she would close her eyes for just a minute...

"Lydia?"

Lydia felt a soft hand on her shoulder, shaking her awake. Her grandmother stood over her, still in her fast-food uniform. Lydia didn't quite follow. She had just laid her head down a minute ago.

"What are you doing home so early?"

"How long have you been sleeping? It's almost six-thirty."

Lydia jumped up, nearly knocking over one of the bags of groceries now covering the table. She must have fallen asleep.

"And look at all this!" Her grandmother brought one last bag in from the hallway and set it down with a clunk on the kitchen table. She pointed to at least a dozen bags, now piled all over. Each one was stuffed with good things: canned peaches, a large ham, cranberries…

"I've never tasted these before." Lydia brought the can closer to see. Unreal. Everything looked so…

"And look here!" Her grandmother pulled out a large frozen bird. "Not just one turkey…two!"

Two turkeys! It was easy to dance about the kitchen, giggling at each new discovery, pulling out packages of marshmallows and spaghetti, canned tuna and sweet potatoes. So many strange foods. Did all Americans eat like this?

"A feast!" her grandmother cried, but then she stopped and looked Lydia in the eye. "But tell me the truth—you didn't hear?"

"I didn't even hear you come in."

"Then who brought all this? It was all left outside the door."

Lydia had no clue, except that she'd heard church groups sometimes delivered groceries to needy families during the holidays. And they, it seemed, were one of those needy families. But when she looked at her grandma, they both smiled at the same time. For a moment they felt more like sisters than grand-mother and granddaughter, *abuela* and *nieta*.

"Are you thinking what I'm thinking?" Lydia asked, and her grandmother nodded her head.

"I think so. We each take a bag, and come back for more."

"One bag for each house?"

That would be fine, so they pulled cans and hams from one bag to the other, spreading out the gifts they would take to oth-ers who were less fortunate than they.

God had given them this food for a reason, had he not? And this would be part of the answer to their prayers.

Lydia couldn't keep the grin from her face as they hurried out into the cold, driving rain. Now it didn't matter.

"Which house first?" she asked as they hurried down the street. That would not be the hard part. The hard part was get-ting away from the families who discovered them before they could get away. One older woman started crying and wanted them to come into her tiny apartment.

"Thank you, no." Lydia's abuela smiled and held her granddaughter's hand. "We have more to deliver before it gets too late, and we're far from home. But…"

She paused, and Lydia filled in what they had already told a handful of other families. How much they loved Jesus, and how he had answered their prayers. Each time she said it to someone new, she felt a little less shy. He had given them so much, even before the groceries; otherwise, she knew, they would not be doing this.

And for the first time, Lydia knew it was really true. The old woman looked at them with tears in her eyes.

"But we just want you to know…," Lydia added, and it wasn't as hard to say now as it was the first time. "We want you to know how much Jesus loves you."

They left the old woman watching them through the window, and Lydia paused for a moment outside an older mobile home, looking something like the *Titanic* in its last moments. A dog growled from the darkness.

"Here?" Lydia wondered, still holding a grocery bag with their one remaining turkey. Her grandmother looked back at her with concern on her face. But Lydia didn't wait, just pushed open the gate and threaded her way past parts of a junk car as she walked up to the door. The dog went wild behind the door when she knocked.

"Anybody home?" She tried again, but no one came to the door. This would be one of the times they would just leave the bag of groceries on the front step and hope for the best. Oh, well. Lydia headed back down the walkway and almost reached the street when she heard a door squeak open. She turned around to find a girl standing in the light of the doorway, her blond hair framed in the light.

Lydia couldn't move. A streetlight flickered overhead, just bright enough to show the girl inside. So this was where Mandy Witherspoon lived. Finally Lydia backpedaled enough to leave the yard.

"Merry Christmas." Lydia forced the words from her mouth, though it wasn't quite as hard as she thought. "And… Jesus loves you, Mandy."

The "Case" Books for Kids

   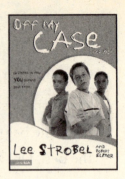

Based on Lee Strobel's Gold Medallion Award–winning *The Case for Christ, The Case for Faith,* and *The Case for a Creator.*

Now those eye-opening bestsellers have been revised by noted children's author Rob Suggs for young people ages eight to twelve—the age when kids begin asking the complicated questions adults themselves struggle to answer. With a companion book—by prolific kids' author Robert Elmer—that gives real-life examples of ways to defend Christianity, these "Case" for books are just right for kids who want to stand up for their faith in an unbelieving world.

Written in humorous, light-hearted prose perfect for kids this age, these books analyze the evidence and build compelling cases using historical facts, up-to-date scientific research, and true stories.

- *The Case for Christ for Kids* brings Jesus to life, addressing the miracles, ministry, family, and way of life of Jesus of Nazareth.

- *The Case for Faith for Kids* explains the most abstract articles of faith in ways kids understand.

- *The Case for a Creator for Kids* uses science to strengthen kids' faith, demystifying the creation of the universe with scientific evidence.

- For kids who are sure of their faith but not sure how to defend it, *Off My Case for Kids*—a perfect companion or a stand-alone piece—provides twelve real-life scenarios that empower kids to speak up when challenged.

Each book has plenty of visual interest, using line illustrations, callouts to define terms and phrases, and sidebars to help explain complicated concepts.

The Case for Christ for Kids

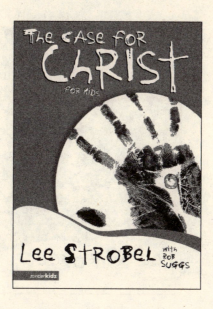

Journalist Lee Strobel analyzed the evidence and built a compelling case for the existence of Jesus. Now his bestselling book has been revised—with kid-friendly terms, humor, and illustrations—to help kids really understand the life and times of Jesus Christ.

SOFTCOVER ISBN 0-310-71147-9

Available at your local bookstore!

The Case For Faith For Kids

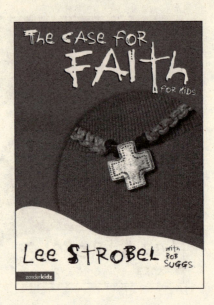

Based on *The Case for Faith*, this inspirational edition for kids ages eight to twelve develops the case for having faith in God. Using words kids understand, coupled with humor, sidebars, and more, *The Case for Faith for Kids* helps kids gain an understanding of what having faith really means.

SOFTCOVER ISBN 0-310-71146-0

Available at your local bookstore!

Off My Case for Kids

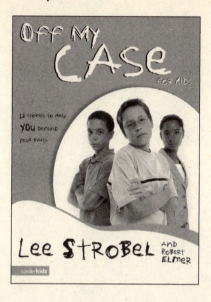

A great companion book or for use all by itself, *Off My Case for Kids* presents twelve real-life scenarios to help kids visualize how they might defend their faith when challenged by unbelievers. Also suggests nonconfrontational ways to handle it, as well as Scripture memory and journaling pages to help put thoughts in their own words.

SOFTCOVER ISBN 0-310-71199-1

Available at your local bookstore!

We want to hear from you. Please send your comments about this book to us in care of zreview@zondervan.com. Thank you.

Grand Rapids, MI 49530
www.zonderkidz.com

zonderkidz

ZONDERVAN.COM/
AUTHORTRACKER

JOURNAL
OF
THE UNKNOWN PROPHET

FOR THE TESTIMONY OF JESUS
IS THE SPIRIT OF PROPHECY.
REVELATION 19:10 NKJV

Legacy to a Renegade Generation

◆ CONTENTS ◆

◆ VOLUME ONE - MERCY ◆

◆ VOLUME TWO - THE ENDTIME MINISTRY ◆

◆ VOLUME THREE - THE CHURCH OF THE LAST AGE ◆

◆ VOLUME FOUR - JUDGEMENT ◆

Foreword

This book is a prophetic work for our time.

The Journal of the Unknown Prophet is one of the few prophetic books that I have read that truly reflects a union of both the Word and the Spirit. Both the spirit and the content of the Journal's prophecies are faithful to the Scriptures and I found a great deal of divine encouragement and guidance in these pages.

I believe the prophecies not only to be true but also to be relevant for our times. The beginning of the Last Days ministry is already here. A cataclysmic outpouring of the Holy Spirit has begun. We are already seeing great signs and wonders. We are beginning to see God's judgement upon His own house. We will soon see stadiums all over the world filled with spiritually hungry people pursuing God, and He will reward their pursuit. His judgements will purify His Bride and make her more attractive and powerful than any other time in history. The Journal reveals to us some of God's intentions as to how He will accomplish this.

Although the Journal can be read at a single sitting, it is not intended to be read this way. Read it prayerfully, letting the power of the message find a home in your heart. Read it in the light of the Scriptures, grounding your beliefs in the more sure Word and in doing so, I believe that you will find much in the book that is profitable for your soul.

The author, Wendy Alec, is a dear friend of mine. I so appreciate her humility, and her passion for the Lord Jesus. Her sensitivity to the Lord's voice and her desire to promote His glory rather than her own ministry, helps her to communicate skilfully the message of the Last Days Revival. My hope is this book will alert many to the urgency of the hour and will bring both repentance and a deeper hunger for being in the presence of the living God.

Dr Paul Cain
President, Shiloh Ministries, Kansas City, Missouri, USA

Dedication

This book is dedicated to Jesus Christ—the fairest of ten thousand—to the immortal, the invisible, to the One who never fails. One day when our work on Earth is complete, we will look into that glorious face and those eyes—those eyes that hold the mercy and the compassion of the ages in their depths.

It is dedicated to the glorious Holy Spirit—to the One who walks beside and within us day after day as we dwell here—for surely it is He who is the voice of the Father and the Son. For He is our wisdom, He is our counsel, He is the great edifier and the encourager of our soul—and it is He who is the revealer of the Father's secrets in this time.

But nothing can compare—nothing upon Heaven and Earth can ever compare to the glorious One—the Creator of Heaven and Earth, our Glorious Father. He who is immortal—He who is omnipotent—God only wise, almighty, inaccessible and hid from our eyes.

May His Kingdom come. May His will be done on Earth as in Heaven. To Him be all worship, all majesty and to Him be all the glory, for ever and ever.

Amen

Introduction

The prophetic writings contained in this Journal were received on three specific occasions, the first being over ten days in the Autumn of 1999, the second in the Spring of 2000 and the third in January of 2002. On account of recent events unfolding on the world stage, we felt it important that the babylon prophecies were accurately dated.

The presence of the lord jesus christ was so tangibly manifest at these times. his terrible grief for his church and those here on earth, mingled with his great mercy and compassion, almost overwhelmed me. but by far, precious reader, his most compelling cry was that of his indescribable love and adoration for his father that we too might know him.

There are many subjects addressed through these pages and in the editorial process, we seriously considered splitting up the journal into different sections, but we felt checked by the holy spirit that it was to remain as one work.

My prayer, dear friend, is that His Holy Spirit will be your guide as your eye falls upon what the Master would impart to you in these crucial endtime days.

Wendy Alec

Across the chasm of eighteen hundred years Jesus Christ makes a demand which is beyond all others difficult to satisfy. He asks for that which a philosophy may often seek in vain at the hands of his friends, or a father of his children, or a bride of her spouse, or a man of his brother. He asks for the human heart: He will have it entirely to Himself; He demands it unconditionally, and forthwith His demand is granted. Its powers and faculties become an annexation to the empire of Christ. All who sincerely believe in Him experience that supernatural love towards Him. This phenomenon is unaccountable, it is altogether beyond the scope of man's creative powers. Time, the great destroyer, can neither exhaust its strength nor put a limit to its range.

NAPOLEON BONAPARTE

Foreword

For as we enter the twenty-first century, there is a cry that would ring out from Jesus Christ of Nazareth, as He who neither slumbers nor sleeps, walks even today through the streets of London, Rome, New York, Beirut, Los Angeles, Delhi, His cheeks wet with tears for a lost and fatherless generation neither cognizant of His presence nor caring.

◆

But still He walks ... unseen ...

and still He weeps ...

For He is still the One who walks, His hands outstretched to the meek and the lowly.

Still He walks, listening out for the cry of the human heart. For where the world has drowned out your cry in its obsessive grasping for success and power and sway, it is to you He comes.

Oh and how long has He sought you, beloved? How many nights, has He stood listening, silently waiting in the shadows unseen by you and those that surround you?

For it was He who wept as He heard your soundless scream in the midnight hour. It was He who watched as you tried in your brokenness to marshall together the fragments of your shattered heart.

And so most beloved of His children, now He comes closer, the fairest of ten thousand. And as He walks out from behind the shadows and you lift up your tear-stained face to Him, half blinded by the radiance from that most beautiful of countenances, He reaches out His hand to you.

He reaches out His hand to touch your face and His touch lingers on your cheek as He brushes away the tears that flow. And He smiles that most wondrous of smiles.

'You?' you mouth soundlessly.

And you hear His tender whisper: I have sought you all your life. Through all the pain, through the loneliness, I have sought you. Each time your heart broke soundlessly with the agony of not belonging, I sought you. Through each rejection, through each hour of despair, I sought you. I was there, loving you. Reaching out to you. It was Me all along.

And as your eyelids gently close as you are engulfed in His tender embrace and the tears fall, somewhere through the sands of time in that netherland betwixt sleeping and waking, you recognise that familiar presence and you too know that He was there. It was He all along.

This is His cry

Volume One

◆ MERCY ◆

JESUS AND THE WOMAN TAKEN IN ADULTERY
JOHN 8:6-7

Volume One

To the men and women who have struggled,
been oppressed, abused, misunderstood.

To those who are lonely, feel passed over,
bereaved, bound, backslidden, discouraged, suicidal.

His mercies in this last age are so near you.
His compassion for you is unbounded. He would
reach out His arms to you and tenderly whisper
your name and draw you apart from the stresses
and strains of twenty-first-century living. For your
struggles are seen of Him and where so often in this
present Church age, His body has failed to take up
your cause and has passed you over, His hands are
outstretched to you, for surely you are not
forgotten by Him.

◆

. . . He is the greatest influence in the world today. There is, as it has been well said, a fifth gospel being written—the work of Jesus Christ in the hearts and lives of men and nations.

G. THOMAS

◆ MERCY ◆

Foreword

It is no coincidence that these words are in your hands. Maybe they have caught your attention on the shelf . . . Maybe you have sought them out or perhaps they are a gift from a loved one. But by whichever route they came to be yours, be assured of this: that the Father Himself tenderly loves you, that the Master has seen into your heart and has known your circumstance and that just for a few moments He would draw you into His presence, into that secret place where His voice is made clear amidst the strains and stresses of twenty-first-century living.

◆

That He would take this opportunity to speak His comfort to your heart, encouragement to a weary soul, refreshing to His faithful servants who labour for Him often unseen and unrecognised by the standards of the Church at present.

◆

He would draw the hurt and misunderstood, the oppressed and the struggling. He would whisper to you: All is well My child, for your deliverer is here. He is mighty in your midst. He would take the hand of the one in the wilderness—in the desert place where all seems barren, where His voice is silent—take your hand and whisper: Don't give up My child; yet a little while and My light shall arise upon you.

He would take the minister, weary of toil and whisper: Well done, Oh faithful one. Your labour for My Gospel is not unseen. Your toil is not for nought. He would take the self-sufficient and with gentle rebuke He would admonish you for putting such stock in your own talent and strength and tenderly He would whisper: Apart from Me, ye are nothing. And He would draw you close, that you might know that your works are but a shadow in His sight.

And to you, so judged and misunderstood, He would draw you close and whisper: That where you have counted to no man, beloved, you are of exceeding more value than rubies to Him. That where no man takes you up He comes with His mighty arm of mercy and compassions. For the Master Himself would whisper to your heart . . .

Dearly beloved, you are not forgotten.

Beloved, I know that it has seemed a desert place.

I have seen your hands fall in despair even when no man has seen. And I have heard your voice cry out to Me, even in the midnight hour, when no man knew or thought that you were in pain.

I have seen the grieving of your heart when no one knew that you had grief to bear. And so My child, I would say to you this day, that as you have walked with Me month after month, year after year in humility, in faithfulness, where you have worshipped Me and adored Me behind closed doors where no man has seen—I would say to you this day—that where no man has seen, surely I, the Lord your God, your redeemer, your Father and your counsellor, that I have seen your heart. I have seen into the depths to the motives and intents of your heart.

Oh beloved, I see you as you worship Me, even in this time of darkness. Oh My child, I see you as you cling to Me even in this time of mundaneness where each day goes by so slowly. You have worshipped Me in spirit and in truth, you have brought great joy to Me when you have drawn near in My presence and have asked nothing but to commune with Me—for surely you have blessed the heart of My Father.

For you see, My child, you have come into My presence wanting to give to Me. You have come into My presence not wanting to take or to gain but to worship Me, to adore Me and to glorify My name.

And so, My child, the Father Himself would gather you as His great treasure, a pearl beyond value, priceless—for as you have placed His fellowship and the fellowship of His Spirit above worldly riches, above human gain, above recognition or power—so surely you have touched the heart of the Father.

And so I would say to you, that even as you have been faithful in the desert place, so in but a short while, there is coming a season upon you and your ministry, upon you and your family, where the rose shall bloom. A season where the bare branches shall bud forth.

A season where rivers shall spring forth in the desert and streams shall flow, where My hand shall move with greater power upon you and in time to come I shall pour out My Spirit in greater measure upon you, that men and women shall say, 'Surely the hand of the Lord God Jehovah is upon you.'

And so it is that doors shall open to you, that divinely ordained opportunities shall come to you. And in that day, you shall rejoice in your heart and know that, I, the Lord your God, am the rewarder of those who seek Me, the rewarder of those who love My presence.

I will open rivers in high places, and fountains in the midst of the valleys; I will make the wilderness a pool of water, and the dry land springs of water.
Isaiah 41:18 KJV

Oh beloved, I see you in that place of solitude.

I see you in that place where no man knows or discerns the call and the destiny or purpose for your life. And I would say to you this day that even in this place, is it not I who have hidden you in the cleft of the rock? Is it not by My sovereign hand that for a brief moment I have chosen to hide My plan and My purpose from those who presently surround you?

You see, beloved child, called out by Me, chosen and ordained to My endtime purpose, it is in the place of solitude, it is in the place of misrepresentation, it is in the place of misunderstanding, it is in the place where you are passed over that I prove you. It is in this place of no recognition and no man's approval that surely your heart is tried and tested as to whom you will serve. So precious child, this day I ask you, would you serve man and man's recognition and obtain man's reward, so fleeting, like a vapour?

Oh no, My child, be strong, be of great courage and draw into My secret place. And it is as you humble yourself even amidst the pain of death to your flesh, even when no man knows your call, when no man sees your place nor discerns My purpose for your life, that it is in the crucible of all that seems to count so much, that truly you are crucified with Me.

That it may be no longer that you live but that My Spirit shall live within you. For surely it shall be that in these coming days My Bride shall say, 'No longer Christ in me, but it is I in Christ. No longer Christ in me, but surely I have been crucified with Christ and my life is hid in Him.'

And so beloved child, in this place of quietness, in this place of obscurity, be not dismayed at all that surrounds you at this present time. But rejoice in that the King is your great right hand and know that as you worship Me and Me alone that I shall bring your purpose forth in season. And that you shall know that to serve the living God and to wait only for My approval and seek only My recognition, that the way of death to self is surely the only way to eternal life in My Kingdom. So be strong, beloved. Be of good courage for I will never fail you nor forsake you. For surely, you have been tried in the furnace of affliction and have been found faithful

I HAVE BEEN CRUCIFIED WITH CHRIST (IN HIM I HAVE SHARED HIS CRUCIFIXION); IT IS NO LONGER I WHO LIVE, BUT CHRIST THE MESSIAH LIVES IN ME; AND THE LIFE I NOW LIVE I LIVE BY FAITH IN (BY ADHERENCE TO AND RELIANCE ON AND COMPLETE TRUST IN) THE SON OF GOD, WHO LOVED ME AND GAVE HIMSELF UP FOR ME.
GALATIANS 2:20
THE AMPLIFIED BIBLE

and so you have touched the heart of the Father.

Oh beloved, how My heart has grieved as I have watched you grasp to defend yourself from those who would seek to attack you.

Oh My child, how I have yearned for you as I have heard you whisper against these same. For what you say is true, but it is in your very choice to become a part of their exposure and of their downfall, that surely you seek your own life and therefore you lose that higher life that you have found in Me.

For surely beloved, I tell you that as you seek and strive to preserve your own, you shall lose it. And as you seek and strive to vindicate yourself, you become once again ensnared.

And as you uncover and propogate your enemy's error—even though what you have found to be, may indeed be true—you yourself become merely a pawn in the hand of the enemy. For I have watched as you have consoled yourself in your enemy's discomfort. And I have watched as you have verified to yourself your anger and justified your reactions against those who would seek your harm. But beloved, this day, I would stretch My arms out to you and call you gently, Oh so gently, to console you. Not in your own vindication or your enemy's exposure, but in Me.

And how My heart grieves for you, beloved, as I watch you lash out in your wretched fears and insecurities against those who have done you wrong. But I tell you, My child, that even amidst the pain and suffering of betrayal—that it is only as you give up your rights to vindicate yourself, that it is only in laying down the injustices, that it is only in forgiving those who have wronged you—that you lay down your life.

And as you lay down your rights, beloved, and as you lay down the fear and the insecurity, and as you stop in your futile attempts to defend all you hold dear—so the torment shall cease and the peace shall arise and you shall find that that which you were unable to protect, when it is given into My hands—I will protect.

No weapon that is formed against thee shall prosper; and every tongue that shall rise against thee in judgement thou shalt condemn. This is the heritage of the servants of the Lord, and their righteousness is of me, saith the Lord. Isaiah 54:17 KJV

And that as you lay down your life, truly you will find it. And that as you pour out a blessing upon those who have spitefully used you—upon those who have abused you, upon those who seek your life and your reputation—you will become free.

And so beloved, when you are so weak and so vulnerable but relying upon Me, then you are made truly strong. So lose your life, My child. Dare to lose your life and you shall gain that higher thing which is life and peace and communion in Me.

Dearly beloved, I know you are weary.

I see you so worn down with the cares and the pressures of each day, that you have almost lost sight of My hand upon your life. Oh beloved, as you enter the end of the age, so shall the pressures increase, so shall your need for times of refreshing become more desperate. For you see, without Me, you are nothing.

Apart from Me you are able to do nothing. In your own strength, in your own power, you will be continually frustrated and unable to accomplish all you have need of. For it is only in a vital continual union with Me, as the source of your life, that you shall in these endtimes be able to survive.

And so, I am drawing you to a place where I will be your very breath, where communion with Me will be your very reason for existence each day, where nothing less will sustain you. I am drawing you to a deeper place in the Spirit where your need for My presence will be so consuming that unless you draw close to Me, the cares and the stresses of life, even of My call upon you, will overwhelm you.

For you see, beloved, I called you to abide in Me. The Father and I seek for those in these times with whom We can make Our abode. We seek worshippers in spirit and in truth. We seek those who hunger for Our fellowship.

We seek those who thirst for Our presence. And through these ones, through this communion, so shall Our presence overflow through My body in the great works prophesied. So shall Our life manifest in greater miracles, in greater healings, in greater exploits, in greater evangelism, in greater conviction of sin than has yet ever been released upon the Earth.

So come, come My child. Come, come My minister. You who are weary, come to Me. For I am your rest, I am your refreshing, I am your anointing, I am your all.

Hast thou not known? Hast thou not heard, that the everlasting God, the Lord, the Creator of the ends of the earth, fainteth not, neither is weary? There is no searching of his understanding. He giveth power to the faint; and to them that have no might he increaseth strength. Even the youths shall faint and be weary, and the young men shall utterly fall; But they that wait upon the Lord shall renew their strength; they shall mount up with wings as eagles; they shall run and not be weary; and they shall walk and not faint. Isaiah 40:28-31 KJV

Oh beloved, so tangled, so ensnared.

Oh beloved, so trapped, so tossed this way and that, I know your thoughts, I read your very inner man. I know the sin that has entangled you in its vicelike grip. My child, I know that you feel you will never be free from its grasp. But My child—you who know My name, you who in the past have experienced My love, My power—is My hand so shortened that I cannot deliver you?

'Yes,' you say, 'but My God, I am in the grip of this thing, I do not want to be free. This sin has become My life.' And I would say to you: beloved child, tempted, tossed and turned, you are the reason I died, you are the one that I love.

Come, come to Me I implore you. Come to Me and I will set you free, that even your end days shall be more glorious and more radiant than your beginning.

Come, come. Draw away from the lies and the snares of the evil one. My precious child, come home to Me. For My child, I have watched you battle with your mind, your thoughts, your flesh.

Oh My child, I have watched you walk in victory for a day and fail the next. But this very day My child, this day My Spirit is upon you to deliver you from the bondages and the snares and entrapments that have so assailed you and today I declare: Freedom, freedom,

One of the Pharisees asked him over for a meal. He went to the Pharisee's house and sat down at the dinner table. Just then a woman of the village, the town harlot, having learned that Jesus was a guest in the home of the Pharisee, came with a bottle of very expensive perfume and stood at his feet, weeping, raining tears on his feet. Letting down her hair, she dried his feet, kissed them, and anointed them with the perfume. When the Pharisee who had invited him saw this, he said to himself, 'If this man was the prophet I thought he was, he would have known what kind of woman this is who is falling all over him.'

Jesus said to him, 'Simon, I have something to tell you.'

'Oh? Tell me.'

'Two men were in debt to a banker. One owed five hundred silver pieces, the other fifty. Neither of them could pay up, and so the banker cancelled both debts. Which of the two would be more grateful?'

Simon answered, 'I suppose the one who was forgiven the most.'

'That's right,' said Jesus. Then turning to the woman, but speaking to Simon, he said, 'Do you see this woman? I came to your home; you provided no water for my feet, but she rained tears on my feet and dried them with her hair. You gave me no greeting, but from the time I arrived she hasn't quit kissing my feet. You provided nothing for freshening up, but she has soothed my feet with perfume. Impressive, isn't it? She was forgiven many, many sins, and so she is very, very grateful. If the forgiveness is minimal, the gratitude is minimal.'

Luke 7:1-12 The Message

freedom. I break the chains that would surround your mind. I break the chains that would fetter your flesh and I, the Most High God, declare to you, that even today, your freedom is in your grasp.

And as you weep before Me, surely My great mercies and My compassions shall yet overshadow you.

My blood shall cleanse you from all iniquity, and the shackles of sin, that have so bound you, shall shatter.

And so like Lazarus you shall come forth, having been dead, yet you shall once more live. And others who have been ashamed and entrapped and entombed shall be drawn to your light and your liberty and many, many shall be liberated by your freedom.

> DO YOU SEE THIS WOMAN? I CAME TO YOUR HOME; YOU PROVIDED NO WATER FOR MY FEET, BUT SHE RAINED TEARS ON MY FEET AND DRIED THEM WITH HER HAIR. YOU GAVE ME NO GREETING, BUT FROM THE TIME I ARRIVED SHE HASN'T QUIT KISSING MY FEET. YOU PROVIDED NOTHING FOR FRESHENING UP, BUT SHE HAS SOOTHED MY FEET WITH PERFUME. IMPRESSIVE, ISN'T IT? SHE WAS FORGIVEN MANY, MANY SINS, AND SO SHE IS VERY, VERY GRATEFUL. IF THE FORGIVENESS IS MINIMAL, THE GRATITUDE IS MINIMAL.

And many shackles shall be shattered by your testimony.

And you shall lift your hands to Heaven and rejoice in the great victory over the hosts of hell that once were your master, for surely beloved, nothing can separate you from My unceasing love.

Nothing shall separate you again away from My side. For My love and My sacrifice for you are stronger than death and are stronger than any hold sin seeks to have over you.

So grasp My hand, beloved, and surely, hand in hand with Me, the great master of eternity, you shall indeed overcome.

I see you, beloved. I see you as you face the endless drudgery of the days that never seem to end.

I watch you, as you struggle from day to day trying to make ends meet, struggling for your very survival alone in your household. I was there when the screaming never stopped, when you sat staring sightlessly thinking that if this was life, you couldn't face tomorrow or the weeks ahead . . . Yet still you carried on, not for your sake, but for the sake of the little ones dependent on you.

I was there as the years passed by and your dreams and ideals, one by one, withered away until one morning you woke up and, looking in the mirror, knew that life as you knew it had passed you by. But there is One who has never passed you by. Oh yes, beloved, there were many times that you felt that I had abandoned you. But

> *For though the mountains shall depart and the hills be shaken or removed, yet my love and kindness shall not depart from you, nor shall my covenant of peace and completeness be removed, says the Lord, Who has compassion on you.*
> *Isaiah 54:10*
> *The Amplified Bible*

My child—never, never have I abandoned you, I have been there, My arms outstretched to you as you sobbed when you felt there was no end to your pain. And even as the following day, your situation eased and help came from an unexpected quarter, Oh beloved child, did you not see My hand? For I had heard your cry and I had seen your tears and My great compassions were near to you, and My mercy overshadowed you.

And so I would say to you, that even at this present time, when all seems dark and hope seems so far from sight, I, the Lord God of Israel would say to you that your face is ever before Me and that I am with you day and night. For I tell you My child that even the years that have seemed so fruitless in your past, that as you call upon My name, that as you stretch your hands out to Me, beloved, that you shall know the comfort of My Spirit and the warmth of My presence. For surely where so many others have forgotten and forsaken you, I the Lord God of Israel, I have not forsaken you. No, I have not forgotten you.

And even this day, as you ask Me to help you, there shall be a joy and a lightness welling up in your heart that you have not experienced for many many years. For you see, My child, as I was with you in your youth, surely I am calling you back to Myself. And through all the years of heartache in the past I give you a fresh hope and a future ahead of you. For surely I am the God of the desolate, I am the God of those who have no hope, for indeed I Myself will be your hope and I Myself will take up your cause. And even in the weeks and the months to come, you shall look back and rejoice and see that I am your Saviour, your mighty deliverer and that all who look to Me, their faces shall indeed be radiant and they shall not be ashamed.

Oh beloved, I have watched as I have seen your heart break with loss and the tears that you could not keep from falling.

For I grieve as I watch your pain. Oh, My child, as you stretch out your hand and fall into My embrace, your agony of heart and soul shall ease. For surely I am He who is the comforter and even in the natural when it seems as though all natural comfort eases not, surely I say to you, beloved, that as you draw close to Me amidst this pain of loss, that I shall put a shield across your heart and that I, My Spirit, the Comforter, shall bathe your heart in His embrace.

AND GOD WILL WIPE AWAY EVERY TEAR FROM THEIR EYES; THERE SHALL BE NO MORE DEATH, NOR SORROW, NOR CRYING. THERE SHALL BE NO MORE PAIN, FOR THE FORMER THINGS HAVE PASSED AWAY.
REVELATION 21:4 NKJV

That even as you have not believed that there could be any rest from the aching in your heart, surely My child, I tell you that as you fling yourself on Me, you shall even experience a supernatural healing, a supernatural comfort that is far beyond and above all earthly solace.

Oh, come to Me, My child, for yet a little while. Do you not yet realise that your timespan on Earth is but a vapour in comparison to eternity? And that once again you shall see your beloved one's face. For surely I tell you, there is no loss here, no sickness, or mourning, for the old order of all things has passed away, only continual light, love and the worship of My Father remain.

So run into My outstretched arms, beloved. Climb into My embrace, and as you place your head upon My heart, allow My supernatural comfort and healing to ease the continual ache in your heart. And precious child, know that even as I speak to you amidst your pain, that your beloved looks upon My face—that they will never again be apart from Me. So you see beloved, while you grieve, they are radiant with the light and the glory and radiance of the joys of Heaven and closeness to Me and My Father.

And know My child, that indeed when your time is come and you shall see Me face to face, so indeed they shall welcome you with Me into the glories that await you here beyond eternity. So do not let your heart be sick any longer, beloved, but lose yourself in My embrace and find comfort for your aching heart.

◆ RUN TO ME ◆

Oh how I love your presence, My child.

Oh how I love to walk and talk with you, beloved.
Oh how I long for you to come and sit with Me at My feet.
Oh how I love your voice.
Oh how I love your presence, My child.

Oh how I long for you to come and sit with Me at My feet. Oh how I love your voice. How I have yearned for your companionship. Oh My child, how I long to fellowship with you.

Oh My child, how My heart has grieved for you as I have watched you run from Me when I would gather you to Me in My arms.

My child, beloved child, I am He who would bless you. I am He who would comfort you. I am He who would talk with you.

I have seen you in your darkness, in your hurt, in your misunderstanding. But I know your heart, My child. I know your heart.

Run to Me in the storms of life. Run into My arms and I will embrace you and wash away the cares and pains of the world that the evil one would inflict on you. Take heart, My child. Your way is not unseen of Me. I am mighty. I am your deliverer. I will yet rejoice over you with singing.

And even in those times when you have failed Me, when you do not feel worthy, My arms are stretched out to you saying: Come, come. Run to My arms.

For it is truly only in My embrace that you will lose sight of yourself and as you look into My face, the entanglements of this world shall fade away. So come into My arms, beloved. Run to Me.

Seek, inquire for, and require the Lord while He may be found (claiming Him by necessity and by right); call upon Him while He is near.

Isaiah 55:6 The Amplified Bible

Oh beloved, how I have yearned to embrace you as I have watched your heart rent with the pain of rejection from one who once held you as their loved one, the only object of their affections.

For My child, I have been with you when no man knew the rending of heart and the pain you endured. And as the words like poisoned arrows were flung back and forth, so I was there standing, weeping for you both, watching you, My heart heavy with grief for you.

FOR WITH GOD NOTHING IS EVER IMPOSSIBLE AND NO WORD FROM GOD SHALL BE WITHOUT POWER OR IMPOSSIBLE OF FULFILMENT.
LUKE 1:37
THE AMPLIFIED BIBLE

And so it is that even at this time, as you have lain on your bed, your pillow soaked night after night, I would walk towards you through the pain and agony of rejection and of despair and I would stretch out My hand to you, your Saviour, your deliverer, your comforter. And Oh yes, My child, yes My beloved, I hear the anguish of your soul crying out: Comfort, there is no comfort! And so I would take your face gently in My hands and I would brush away the tears from your cheek and I would adjure you: Is My hand so shortened to save? Am I not still the miracle-working God of Abraham, Isaac and of Jacob? For I tell you this day My child, I admonish you this day, that where those around you have said it is too hard, it is over, I would declare to you: Is not a man's heart in My Father's hand? Is a man's heart too far from the conviction of My Spirit?

And so it is that I declare to you, that from this day forth, the battle is no longer yours. So gently disentangle yourself and loose the situation into My hands and the hands of My Father—and as you ease that which you have held so tightly to yourself—so I tell you, My child, that My supernatural rest shall start to flood your soul. And where you have found no ease for your aching heart, and where the pain and agony of rejection and loss has been too much to bear, so I tell you, child, that even from this time, there shall be an easing and a healing and a strength that shall flood over your soul whereas before you were weak with despair. A fresh hope shall infuse you.

For I tell you that as Lazarus was dead, and it seemed that all hope was lost and Mary wept before Me and I was moved, so deeply moved, I tell you this day, I have been moved by the agony of your soul.

Child, am I still
not the same God

impossible?

Child, am I still not the same God of the impossible? The same God that parted the Red Sea? That turned water into wine? That raised Lazarus from the dead? Can My Father not arrest a stone cold heart and bring it back to life in a union that was ordained by Me?

Oh yes My child. For I tell you now that the arrows, the arrows of My Spirit, the conviction of My Spirit, have been loosed by My Father's hand to relentlessly pursue. Oh yes, I pursue your loved ones day and night, for there is a love that will not let them go. And so you shall see, even when those around you did not believe, you shall see a man brought back from rebellion and from lawlessness as one brought back from the dead.

For it is not finished, My child, and where those around you would say, 'Let go, it is finished,' you have known, deep in your heart, that this is not the way that things should be.

For I was born into this world to destroy the works of darkness and to undo the works of Satan and so I say to you: Now be strong. Gird up your loins and behold and see the day of your salvation. For I tell you that there is a miracle in your midst. If you just cling to Me and believe, for surely, beloved, you shall see that the Lord is good and greatly to be praised and adored.

Oh beloved, for I have seen your head bowed down with the heaviness of the cares around you, even that you have lost the will to carry on. For it may have seemed as if there has been no logical plan for your life . . .

. . . I have seen you, My child, as you have continued day by day doing all that you know to do and yet still there seemed to be no breakthrough. And so you became weary in well doing. And after a time your limbs hung down. And indeed your face—which in the past had been radiant when experiencing My presence and My joy—has also become bowed down.

Oh My child, did you think I did not see? Did you think that My hand had passed over you? Oh no, beloved. But you see, there is a time to discern and to understand the times and the seasons in your walk with Me, and many, many of My children, when passing through the aridness of a preparational season in their lives, fail to discern My ways and My purpose ordained for them to bring My ordained and higher purpose to fruition in their lives.

And so when it appears as though there is no growth and no fruit and no manifest sign of My presence or My purpose in their lives, they lose hope and lose courage and so become weary in well doing. And so it is beloved child, that I plead with you this day: Lift up your head, strengthen your weary limbs, for indeed, the waiting process is almost complete.

And yet a little while, yet a little while and your time of harvest shall be at hand. So arise, My child, arise from the depression that circumstances have chained you in and unloose the fetters that bind you and once again, draw close to Me and embrace My presence.

For surely I tell you, that it is only when you take your eyes off My face and turn them back to yourself that in a season of waiting you will be overwhelmed. It is in this time of hardship, it is in this time of fallow ground when all around you seems bare that you must cling to Me and cling to the fellowship of My Holy Spirit.

For beloved, it is only in My presence that you will find the strength and the courage to carry on. And carry on indeed you shall, beloved, for there shall be a great recompense of reward for all who stay the course.

> MY BELOVED SPAKE, AND SAID UNTO ME, RISE UP, MY LOVE, MY FAIR ONE, AND COME AWAY. FOR, LO, THE WINTER IS PAST, THE RAIN IS OVER AND GONE;
> THE FLOWERS APPEAR ON THE EARTH; THE TIME OF THE SINGING OF BIRDS IS COME, AND THE VOICE OF THE TURTLE IS HEARD IN OUR LAND;
> I HAVE SEEN THOSE WHO HAVE BETRAYED YOU, MY CHILD.
> THE FIG TREE PUTTETH FORTH HER GREEN FIGS, AND THE VINES WITH THE TENDER GRAPE GIVE A GOOD SMELL. ARISE, MY LOVE, MY FAIR ONE, AND COME AWAY.
> SONG OF SOLOMON 2:10-13 KJV

So lift up your head, My child, draw into your chamber, for I am with you. I am your lover, I am your great reward, I am your beloved. Come away with Me.

I have seen those who have betrayed you, My child.

I have seen those who behind your back have sought to take that which was yours, which you hold dear. I have watched as they have fallen, each to his and her own lusts as the enemy has enticed them to betray that which was another's. And so, I have seen you, My child, I have seen the tears of pain and hurt as they have fallen in the night hour. I have heard your voice cry out to Me, amidst the pain of betrayal by those you supped with, by those who were once for you, who you considered brothers . . .

And now, beloved, I come to you. As one who has known the pain, as one who has experienced the anguish of brother betraying brother, for surely on the night they sought My very life, I knew the agony of one who was betrayed.

But beloved, I tell you that even now as you sit silently in your pain, I tell you, it is not yours to defend nor vindicate yourself. That it is not yours to react and protect yourself. That it is yours to forgive and to cover over this offence, that it is yours to allow the healing balm of My presence to erase all wrong, for surely I am the great healer of men's hearts. And surely I am the great comforter of men's souls. And so I tell you, My child, that as you run to Me and refuse to vent your hurt and your anger upon the one who betrayed your heart, so I tell you, that I indeed shall be your great right hand.

And child, suddenly you shall see, like the sun, My vindiction rise. And suddenly you shall see My hand move upon your heart and the heart of the one who wronged you. But it is only as you let the wrong that was done against you go, and as you forgive the one who harmed you, that My Spirit can move. But I tell you, My child, that indeed My Spirit shall move and a mighty restoration there shall be.

EVEN MY OWN FAMILIAR FRIEND,

IN WHOM I TRUSTED

(RELIED ON AND WAS CONFIDENT), WHO ATE OF MY BREAD,

HAS LIFTED UP HIS HEEL AGAINST ME.

PSALM 41:9

THE AMPLIFIED BIBLE

Oh beloved, for I have seen as you have suffered, day after day, month after month.

I have seen as you have cried out to Me for healing and yet looking at your body, you have seen no change, you have known no ease. I have seen as in the darkest hours you have cried to Me: Lord, I fear, for it depends on my faith and I have no faith!

And so your heart has been afraid and your hands have hung limp with dread. And beloved child, this day I would comfort you. This day I would declare to you: As you put your hand in Mine, as you put your faith in My person, that beloved child, is faith indeed.

So beloved in this time of anxiety, do not listen to the lies and the snares of the evil one who would whisper to you: You have no faith, there is no hope for you. For I tell you, beloved, I did not call you to have faith in your faith. I did not call you to have faith in healing. I did not call you to have faith and rely and lean on your own strength. But I said to you, I declared to you, that even in your very weakness, I shall show Myself strong on your behalf. And even today beloved, I declare to you that even in your weakest moment, as you reach out your hand to Me—as yet even in the face of the great darkness that surrounds you, you lift up your voice and your heart to Me—so I declare to you, beloved, that this is faith indeed.

For I search not for a people who have faith in a formula. I search

JESUS RAISING UP THE DAUGHTER OF JAIRUS
LUKE 8:54

not for a people who have faith in their own faith. I search not for a people who have faith in a promise book. But I tell you My child, My Father and I seek out a people who have faith in My person, who have faith that I Am.

So surely this day My child, I tell you you DO have faith. As My Father and I watch you, We see a child who is filled with faith, filled with faith, for beloved, you are filled with faith in Me. And so beloved, do not fret.

And so I declare unto you, do not fear. For My Father and I, We run to your aid, We run to your assistance. For did I not say that you only need faith as small as a mustard seed to move mountains. And so this day I tell you that you have faith to be healed, beloved. For you have faith in Me.

For surely this day I declare to you, you have faith to be healed, for you have faith in My Father. And so My healing virtue starts to flow. And so My healing power starts to rise towards you. And so My great compassions start to move towards you. And so My mercies start to overshadow you. For you see, beloved, you do not need faith in miracles, you need faith in the One who works the miracles. You see, beloved, you do not need faith in healing, you need faith in the One who heals. You need faith in the One who spoke the Word—in the One who IS the Word made flesh.

While he yet spake, there cometh one from the ruler of the synagogue's house, saying to him, Thy daughter is dead; trouble not the Master. But when Jesus heard it, he answered him, saying, Fear not: believe only, and she shall be made whole. And when he came into the house, he suffered no man to go in, save Peter, and James, and John, and the father and the mother of the maiden. And all wept, and bewailed her: but he said, Weep not; she is not dead, but sleepeth. And they laughed him to scorn, knowing that she was dead. And he put them all out, and took her by the hand, and called, saying, Maid, arise. And her spirit came again, and she arose straightway: and he commanded to give her meat.

Luke 8:49-55 KJV

And now I declare: See your healer comes towards you, not dependent on your faith in My works, but dependent on your faith in Me. Every satanic curse shall be broken, the spirit of infirmity that has bound you, shall be destroyed. The fetters of disease and sickness shall be broken. And now I release HEALING, HEALING, HEALING. Be loosed from your infirmity. Be loosed from your sickness. Be loosed from your disease. Be loosed from pain. Be healed. Be healed. It is yours.

Be healed.
It is yours.

Beloved child, surrounded by accusation.

Even though all that is within you would seek to vindicate yourself—precious child, seek My face and trust in My vindication—for your efforts to justify and redeem yourself will only lead to sorrow.

In My Word I instructed you to pray for those who spitefully use you. Through all the pain and accusation and misunderstanding of the present, walk in My ways, obey My Word, cling closely to Me and forgive those who seek to destroy you and yours. For surely, I am your fortress, I am your tower of refuge. I am your strong tower and I am your great right hand.

'BUT I SAY TO YOU WHO HEAR: LOVE YOUR ENEMIES, DO GOOD TO THOSE WHO HATE YOU, BLESS THOSE WHO CURSE YOU, AND PRAY FOR THOSE WHO SPITEFULLY USE YOU.

'GIVE TO EVERYONE WHO ASKS OF YOU. AND FROM HIM WHO TAKES AWAY YOUR GOODS DO NOT ASK THEM BACK.

'AND JUST AS YOU WANT MEN TO DO TO YOU, YOU ALSO DO TO THEM LIKEWISE.'
LUKE 6:27-28, 30-31
NKJV

Oh precious child, forgive those who have misjudged you. Oh beloved, they do not discern nor understand My purposes. They do not comprehend nor see through My eyes. For their judgements are not My judgements and their discernments are not My discernments. For they judge externally. They judge on the measure of charisma and of influence and of prosperity.

I say there is coming a time when My ministers shall no longer judge incorrectly but their judgements shall be My judgements. I tell you there is coming a season when their measures shall be My measures. For many, many that I hold dear have in this hour been rejected and passed over by the leaders and those who hold position in this day. For their measures are the measures of the world, the measures of men but My measures are the measures of Heaven.

Come unto me, all ye that labour and are heavy laden, and I will give you rest. Take my yoke upon you, and learn of me; for I am meek and lowly in heart: and ye shall find rest unto your souls. For my yoke is easy, and my burden is light.
Matthew 11:28-30
KJV

For I am gentle and My yoke is easy to bear and I have called you to My divine purpose. And even as you have harkened to My voice and have followed My path, yes beloved, it has been a hard way.

Yes beloved, much of the fruit and the victories you have not yet seen in the natural. But I have called you, I have ordained you to fulfil My purposes in the Earth in this, the final generation.

And it is by My sovereign mighty hand that I have called you. For have I not called you to be a repairer of the breach, a deliverer of the oppressed, to pour yourself upon the nations of this world in this endtime? To glorify My name, to impart My presence, to feed My poor, to teach My Church?

Oh, teach My Church. Teach My Church that they may be One. Feed My Church with the Word that is the Word from My throne, for My Church is weak and oppressed. Many think they thrive but they know not My presence.

Feed My poor, feed My poor, for many of My poor have My presence. Many of My poor know My face yet they perish and they cry out to Me for mercy, but My Church turns their face. My Church does not hear, for My Church feeds only that which benefits themselves, for My Church has become a place of trade, a place of merchandise.

Purify My Church. Purify My House that it may be fit for the Bridegroom, that it may be fit for the Harvest. Purify My Church that My Kingdom may come.

Oh precious beloved child who I love more than life itself.

How My Father and I love to be with you. Even in the business of your serving Me, when you place time aside to fellowship with Us. We hasten to be at your side.

You are Our great desire. For Oh beloved, We search to and fro across the cities and the nations of the Earth searching for those who We can make Our abode with. For so many of My children know Me by name, but they know not My face. For so many of My children know Me by My Word. But beloved they know not My face. But beloved, it is to those who know My face, it is to those who love My appearing that My Father and I will manifest Ourselves.

For My child, you can see Me at any time with the eyes of your heart. For those who worship in spirit and in truth, these are the ones who shall see the Son in His Kingdom in all His glory, for My Kingdom comes in your heart. It is in your heart that the Father and I shall appear to you. And so it is these ones who love Our appearing that are great treasures in Our sight.

For, Oh, there are many, many who serve Us. And there are many who trust in Our Word. There are many who do great works for Us, but I tell you beloved that there is a time coming when My people will know Us in spirit and in truth and those who love Me and My Father, We will draw near to them and We will make Our abode with them.

For these are Our pearls of great price upon the Earth. For many, many want to be used by Me. But I tell you, beloved, it is these who love to be with Me, it is these who love My presence. It is these to whom I am their very breath.

These are My Church, these are My beloved, these are My friends. And as the end of the age draws near, it is to this remnant that I shall reveal My secrets, that the Father shall reveal His secret counsel.

YOU ARE MY FRIENDS WHEN YOU DO THE THINGS I COMMAND YOU. I'M NO LONGER CALLING YOU SERVANTS BECAUSE SERVANTS DON'T UNDERSTAND WHAT THEIR MASTER IS THINKING AND PLANNING. NO, I'VE NAMED YOU FRIENDS BECAUSE I'VE LET YOU IN ON EVERYTHING I'VE HEARD FROM THE FATHER.
JOHN 15.
WORDS OF JESUS,
THE MESSAGE.

And so beloved, My heart has been broken with the things that have broken your heart.

For I see you struggle from one day to the next. I see the tears of despair and the pain of rejection as a spouse rejected and I would say to you: Where no man has known your pain, I the Lord your God have known and I am the One who takes you up. For My arms reach out to you with a burning compassion for you. For surely I know the hardness of men's hearts in these days. And surely My Father and I weep over this fatherless and lawless generation.

And so My child, today, I would draw you tenderly aside and I would draw you out of the loneliness and the despair that surround your day. For I would declare to you, that from this time forth, I do a new thing in your life. Yes, I declare to you this day beloved, that it is time to cast aside what has gone before. For the season has come and gone, and for you, now the past must be put aside.

And beloved, as you determine to forgive in your heart and you forgive those who wronged you, who caused the betrayal of your heart, so I shall once again pour out My Spirit upon you.

For I tell you that there waits for you a fresh season in your life ahead. And I tell you My child, that the weights and agonies of yesteryear shall start to dissolve as you discard the past even as a caterpillar sheds its cocoon and rises to new life. For it is the season to rise from the depression of your circumstances and rise to a fresh season where surely fresh hope shall start to infuse your heart.

For a new day dawns for you, a day liberated from the past and from the pain of rejection. And you shall yet be radiant with the joy of a new life. So take My hand, beloved, and rejoice expectantly, for surely you shall once more be radiant. For I have not forsaken thee nor abandoned thee, and even in these next months, you shall indeed see circumstances change and shift and a great healing shall take place in your heart, so that those around you shall stare at you in wonder and proclaim—is this the same?—for she radiates and shines with new life and with fresh hope.

> To appoint unto them that mourn in Zion, to give unto them beauty for ashes, the oil of joy for mourning, the garment of praise for the spirit of heaviness; that they might be called trees of righteousness, the planting of the Lord, that he might be glorified.
> Isaiah 61:3 KJV

For I tell you, beloved, My destiny still awaits you, My plans for you still stand. Plans to prosper you. Plans for your great deliverance, years of fulfilment and blessing and hope.

Oh no, you have not been forsaken. So take the first steps towards your destiny this day and take My hand and rise up to fresh hope, beloved. For I, the Lord God of Israel, have taken you up.

Take My
hand and rise up
to fresh hope, beloved.
For I,
the Lord God
of Israel,
have taken you up.

Beloved, do you not know? Do you not see? As you seek to find love, it is really Me you are looking for.

And Oh beloved, I tell you that although My Church have upheld the principles of Scripture, so they often have not done with a true reflection of My heart and of My grace. And I would say to you this day—I stand before you with My arms outstretched, not in judgement but in mercy, beloved son, beloved daughter. I stand before you at this moment, not in condemnation but with mercy and with a love that would relentlessly pursue you.

For I was there at the first abuse of your body. I was there when you were mocked and rejected by your peers and a seering came to your sensitive heart—to that same heart that I ordained to love and to reach out and to worship Me. And as the Father of lies whispered to your heart: You are not like other men, you are not like other women, you do not fit . . . you embraced the lies. You indeed drew to yourself others ensnared and battling the same and so the lie took root and the lifestyle was born.

BUT HE WAS WOUNDED FOR OUR TRANSGRESSIONS, HE WAS BRUISED FOR OUR INIQUITIES: THE CHASTISEMENT OF OUR PEACE WAS UPON HIM; AND WITH HIS STRIPES WE ARE HEALED.
ALL WE LIKE SHEEP HAVE GONE ASTRAY; WE HAVE TURNED EVERY ONE TO HIS OWN WAY; AND THE LORD HATH LAID ON HIM THE INIQUITY OF US ALL.
ISAIAH 53:5-6 KJV

For I know the breaches in your soul. I was there when your heart was scarred and bruised where others did not understand. Surely

I am He who sees and who knows. For was I not the recipient of rejections and misunderstanding? Was I not He who was despised and rejected by men? Oh My son, My daughter, forgive My Church. Forgive those who judged you who follow Me. For surely, though they know My Word, they hearken not to the breath of My Spirit. For My voice is quiet, full of tenderness, full of mercy.

And as you seek fulfilment of both the flesh and the soul I would reach out and embrace you and draw you to Myself. And as I would embrace you, I weep for you My son, My daughter. I weep for you and there is no refrain from My tears. For as you transgress the eternal law set in motion by My Father Himself, I weep as I see you bring that which cannot be revoked down upon yourself. For the consequence of breaking the eternal law cannot be revoked. And My judgement upon you is My mercy. Take heed beloved, take heed and hear My voice.

Oh beloved, do you think I do not know, that I cannot see, that you seek the salve of the human heart but it is only to be found in Me. In no other upon Heaven and Earth shall you find the rest for your aching soul.

Oh beloved, you sit before Me and you say it has been too hard, you have no heart left to continue.

But Oh beloved, you cannot in this season look to the temporal. You dare not in this hour focus on those things that presently surround you. For even as it is in the circumstances of this Earth that seem at present so fruitless—and even as the branches in your life seem to be bare and without bud—surely I would tell you that all things around you and outside you, your finances, your work environment, your ministry, your Church situation— and child, even that which you called impossible, even that which no one knows nor guesses nor could imagine . . .

> THOU TELLEST MY WANDERINGS: PUT THOU MY TEARS INTO THY BOTTLE: ARE THEY NOT IN THY BOOK?
> PSALMS 56:8 KJV

I tell you, I am He who walks with you, I am He who is beside you in the midnight hour as much as in the light of the noonday sun. I am He who has seen and who has heard all that that you have kept secretly within your heart and that which your heart has broken over. For I am the God of the secret places in your heart and I alone have seen the tears fall over that which no one guessed, not even those closest to you.

And when you had no strength to bear those secret things, so you found strength in Me. And when you had no reason to carry on, you found meaning and reason in Me. And so beloved, this day I implore you—look up beyond this temporal life to that which is eternal—to that which shall be written in the great and marvellous Book of Life. And seek to be counted in the pages of this wonder. For surely on that great day when the Books are opened and My Father Himself would wipe every tear from your eye and the old order is passed away and all mourning is finished and My Kingdom is come in all its glory—on that day beloved—all that is built on the sands of temporal and earthly things shall be burned up even in a moment as a vapour. But that which you have done for Me, when you felt you had no strength, shall be recorded. And that which you did for another—where there was no gain, but you did in My place on My behalf and in My Name—this shall be recorded.

All your tears weeping for a lost generation, all your prayers seen only in the secret place, all the wounds of battle within this present Church age . . . the scars and the aching of heart and the souls that were saved for My sake . . . and My Gospel that you preached faithfully and unstintingly, even when you were bare and dry, yet you faithfully proclaimed . . . this shall be recorded.

And the poor that you helped and the bowed down that you raised up . . . and the men and women that you took time for and discipled . . . and the encouraging words you gave even when no one encouraged you . . . Oh yes My child, these are the things of your life that shall be written in the Book of Life.

All your tears weeping for a lost
generation . . .
all your prayers seen only
in the secret place . . .
The poor that you helped . . .
The **bowed down**
that you raised up . . .
And the encouraging words
you gave even when
no one encouraged you . . .
Oh yes **My child**,
these are the things of your life
that shall be written in the
Book of Life.

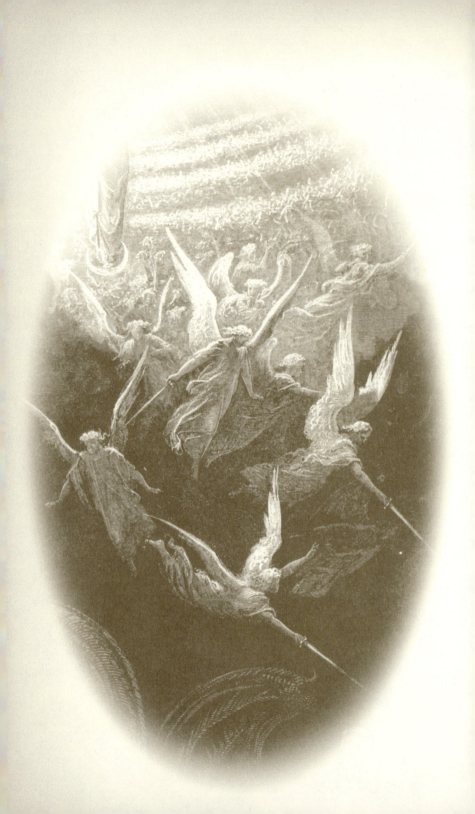

Volume Two

◆ THE ENDTIME MINISTRY ◆

THE VISION OF THE FOUR CHARIOTS
AND THE ANGEL ANSWERED AND SAID UNTO ME: 'THESE ARE THE FOUR SPIRITS OF
THE HEAVENS, WHICH GO FORTH FROM STANDING BEFORE THE LORD OF ALL THE
EARTH.' ZECHARIAH 6:5

Volume Two

To the men and women of valour, who love not their lives unto death.

To these who have received the last great call to fight in the Epic Battle of the Ages as the Bride of Christ stands on the outskirts of the endtime age of the Church.

And so we reach an hour in the Church age where the Spirit of truth and of grace would draw you to Himself that even amidst the myriad pressures and activities of ministry, you might hear that most wonderful of voices speak to your heart with a greater clarity for the coming endtime hour. For surely in all that lies ahead as we enter the final Church age, His voice will be our beacon and our great autopilot as we prepare to fly by instruments in the endtime days approaching.

◆

No great life ever passed so swiftly, so quietly, so humbly, so far removed from the noise and commotion of the world; and no great life after its close excited such universal and lasting interest.

Philip Schaff

Prepare to minister to a different timing in a more accurate measure, for His next age of the Church is the season that will herald in the endtime plan of the Father. For many, many of His ministers have been out of step with Him in this past Church age —many, many of His ministers have been only in His permissive will, doing that which is righteous and is good but that which has often been out of time with His Spirit.

———◆———

For there is a shifting and a changing in the seasons that exist in this present Church age. And the manner in which the Master's servants have ministered in this past season has been a right and a just measure for this season, but surely the Spirit of the Living God would say unto you that the season for the old has passed by and it is time for His ministers, His called-out ones to prepare for a new season, to prepare for a new anointing.

———◆———

For surely it is to His evangelists that the Lord at this time endows a special grace.

And in this season there rises upon these special messengers, God's evangelists, a new and unusual grace—where other members of the fivefold will be judged by the Lord Himself if they attempt to operate in this manner—a peculiar grace in this next dispensation. For the evangelist will be released to operate in what to some may appear as spectacular rather than the supernatural. But it will be from the Spirit of the Living God. And to those evangelists who truly operate in a mandate from the Living God, the supernatural will now start to translate from what has been a mere shadow, into a true multiplication of souls.

For God has heard the cry of His evangelists. He has heard their cry for souls and where previously there has been little true fruit, even though to the laymen it may have appeared plentiful, in this past season, the reaping of souls to the evangelist has been greatly lacking in comparison to the visions of multiplication that these sent ones have been shown by the Holy Spirit at this time.

And so the Church is about to enter a time, when all that has been revealed to the evangelist by the Holy Spirit, those things which have been spoken in secret, those visions which have been received in the inner chambers, that have as yet borne little fruit in the natural, it is in these coming years and dispensation that the evangelist shall truly rise as God's Messenger, as His flames of fire.

And so, a peculiar grace shall rest, that even amid controversy, even amid accusation, that a great drawing power shall start to rest upon God's called-out ones. That even the world shall be moved to look upon them with wonder. And many of the Church shall shake their heads, for in this season the evangelist shall himself start to rise up as an abrasion to the religious spirit that has so dominated the charismatic, pentecostal body.

And so God will allow seemingly peculiar things to arrest the body's attention. Oh yes, says the Spirit of God, those religious ones shall call it spectacular. Oh yes, they shall say it is a vanity, a drawing unto man. But it is a peculiar grace and so there shall be upon My sent ones a multiplication that shall take place. And from the thousands it shall be multiplied to tens of thousands. And from hundreds of thousands to the populations of towns, and then to cities and so it shall be that even whole nations shall be set aflame by the fire and the presence of the Living God.

For My Church has been so complacent. I do not hear the cry for souls. Souls, the Spirit of the Living God cries: Souls. For I am now raising up My latter-day evangelists who have cried to Me: SOULS. I have heard the cry of My evangelists, I have heard the CRY of My sent ones. And they in their inner chambers have cried out to Me: SOULS. And so this day I would say to you, I have heard this cry. I have heard the anguish and My hand comes swiftly to release the Endtime Harvest of souls upon the Earth.

Do not rest you evangelists, says the Spirit of the Living God. Do not rest from your labours. For surely I tell you that up until this time you have but seen a minute portion. You have but seen a fraction of the multitudes of souls that are about to be multiplied to My evangelists.

Preach, preach. Do not rest from your labours. For as you have sown in tears in the secret place believing that you would see this day, so I declare to you that this day is almost upon you. And even at this time, you will sense a very change in the climate of the reaping of the Harvest.

And I am about to do peculiar things, says the Lord. I am about to pour out a peculiar grace upon you. A peculiar grace, even as you have not seen manifested in your ministry before. And so you shall see that as you travel from city to city and from nation to nation, that you shall start to operate in a dimension and in a peculiar grace that shall shake the very core of the hordes of hell. For you shall walk even in a new level of authority in the spirit realm. For you shall be granted power from on high to shake the regions of the damned.

> AND I WILL SHOW YOU WONDERS IN THE SKY ABOVE AND SIGNS ON THE EARTH BENEATH, BLOOD AND FIRE AND SMOKING VAPOUR;
> THE SUN SHALL BE TURNED INTO DARKNESS AND THE MOON INTO BLOOD BEFORE THE OBVIOUS DAY OF THE LORD COMES—THE GREAT AND NOTABLE AND CONSPICUOUS AND RENOWNED (DAY).
> AND IT SHALL BE THAT WHOEVER SHALL CALL UPON THE NAME OF THE LORD (INVOKING, ADORING AND WORSHIPPING THE LORD—CHRIST) SHALL BE SAVED.
> ACTS 2:19-21
> THE AMPLIFIED BIBLE

And in the coming season, a new dispensation of the supernatural shall begin to manifest in your ministry. A fresh outpouring of the supernatural. For yes, you have moved in a true measure of the supernatural but it has been merely a shadow of what lies ahead. For I shall do fearsome and wondrous things that even the elements, that signs and wonders shall manifest, even as the prophets of Baal in the past did their magic and Elijah called down fire from Heaven. So I tell you that in this day and in the season to come, so shall My evangelists move with power and with might. And I shall rain down signs. And I shall rain down wonders, wonders that the world may wonder. Wonders that shall confound the wise. Wonders that will cause major TV broadcasters to come and stare and they shall know that the hand of the Most High God has done this thing.

Prepare for the wonders, My called-out ones. I speak WONDERS. Prepare for My wonders. Prepare for this peculiar move of the spectacular, such as you have not yet seen of the supernatural.

And it is to My teachers in this hour that I would speak a new Word, that I would speak a fresh Word.

For in this past season surely it has been that My teachers have taught My people My Book, that they may know and understand and learn to discern and divide clearly and consistently My Word. But I tell you now that in this latter time, a new anointing shall spring forth and a new outpouring shall fall upon those who have been faithful to feed My sheep in this last hour. And surely I tell you that to those of My teachers who have been found faithful to feed My sheep in this last hour, and to these ones who have not only held to the spirit of the law but to My Holy Spirit—to these there is about to rise a supernatural portion of My anointing to feed My sheep in these coming days.

For there shall start to rise up in those who I anoint as teachers in this next dispensation, a prophetic knowing and a Spirit of revelation that shall increase. And they shall find that in this coming season, as they go to teach My Word, a supernatural outpouring shall start to accompany their words. And that as it has been in the past, that My teachers have moved in the Word, now it shall be that they shall move both fully yoked by My Word and by My Holy Spirit.

And so it shall be that even some of those who have found it hard and a hard yoke to bear, for many of those who are called to teach

My people, many of these who have been true to fulfil their call, at present walk in an aridness in that same call for they have not harkened to the Spirit of God in these times. For My Spirit is drawing them, is drawing them into an outpouring of both My Word and My Spirit. And so it is that I am calling these ones. For surely although they are at present out of time with Me, they have still been found faithful to My person. And so I will now draw them gently into My time frame in the Holy Ghost. For the Word alone is yesterday's manna and even they have seen deep in their hearts, that it is no longer enough to feed My people. And so it is that I will now raise My teachers. That now they will come forth and in this new season they will blossom like a rod that had no bud, and they shall stand before the congregations and I shall start to pour upon them the supernatural that My Word in this season shall be confirmed by My Spirit.

FOR THE WORD ALONE IS YESTERDAY'S
Manna

And so, My prophetic teachers shall rise. They shall teach minute by minute under the unction of My Holy Spirit, they shall open up My Word minute by minute in obedience to My voice. And in this season there shall indeed be a great drawing unto My person. Oh yes, for surely it is in this hour that I call to My teachers to teach My people to feed My sheep the true manna right and on time for this generation, that they might lift up My person that I may draw all men unto Me.

My beloved, now indeed you shall have the great privilege to teach My Bride about Me. That she may abide in Me, that she may draw unto Me. That she may know that without Me, she is nothing. That in this hour it is no longer enough for My teachers to declare to My people: Christ in you. Oh no, but now in this time, it shall be that My sheep, that My Bride has been crucified with Me and that she is hidden in Me.

And so you see, beloved, this is the meat of the Word that you shall teach in these days. And therefore I shall raise My teachers up to prepare My Bride without spot, wrinkle or blemish, in these times. And secondly I would instruct those who are sovereignly called and ordained to be teachers of My Word in this next season: Prepare yourselves. Prepare for a great outpouring of the prophetic upon you, for suddenly as you teach, I shall drop into your spirit a supernatural knowing and you shall hear Me direct you in a different manner than what has gone before in this time, says the Lord.

> AND THE TEACHERS AND THOSE WHO ARE WISE SHALL SHINE LIKE THE BRIGHTNESS OF THE FIRMAMENT, AND THOSE WHO TURN MANY TO RIGHTEOUSNESS (TO UPRIGHTNESS AND RIGHT STANDING WITH GOD) SHALL GIVE FORTH LIGHT) LIKE THE STARS FOREVER AND EVER.
> DANIEL 12:3
> THE AMPLIFIED BIBLE

And so it shall be that in this time you shall move faster, much faster. For there shall be a quickening of My Spirit to those endowed with My teaching gift in these times. And you shall move through My Word here and there, in a manner and pace that you did not previously experience.

And so, My sheep shall be fed. My sheep shall be fed with the finest wheat with a word in season and with the measure of My Spirit.

And now it is as the good shepherd that I would speak to those shepherds in this hour that have been counted faithful and true.

For surely as My eyes run to and fro across the nations of the Earth, in this hour I have found many, many of My shepherds who have been faithful and true stewards of My sheep. How tender My heart is to the pastors that have fed My lambs. And I would speak to My pastors and say: Strengthen, strengthen what remains. Strengthen your tent pegs. Strengthen the stakes that you have dug into the ground of your communities. For yet a little while, yet a little while and you shall see increase. Yet, a short time and you shall see an enlarging of your territories and an increasing in the influence of My Spirit within your neighbourhoods, within your cities, within your communities.

For as you have laboured in hard ground and as you have watered the dry soil and as you have sown your seed under the harshness of the noonday sun, so beloved, today I declare to you—that as you have spent your strength for My lambs and as you have laid your life down for My sheep—so truly I tell you that when it seemed in the midnight hour that there was not one who saw, that there was not one who appreciated, that there was not one who encouraged, that I was with you.

When you fed My sheep I walked with you through the dust and the briers, when you rescued My little ones from the pit of destruction, I held you strong when your limbs were too weary to walk the extra mile. And as you brushed the tears from My lambs, I brushed the tears from your cheeks. And so it is that in this next coming season of My body and in this final Church age, so now My true shepherds shall arise.

They shall arise from the Bronx and they shall arise from the prairies. They shall arise from the inner cities and they shall arise from the capitals. They shall arise from the mega churches and they shall arise from the country.

Now they shall come forth to feed My sheep, they shall come forth to feed My lambs. They shall feed them with that which endures, not just for a season, but for a generation My sheep shall be fed.

And as My shepherds come forth so I shall pour out upon them My very Spirit and so it shall be that My pastors in this day and in this hour shall walk in a greater spirit of revelation—and a greater portion of faith. And as My Spirit of revelation is poured upon them they shall enlarge the places of their vision and prepare for great exploits to impact their cities and their nation. And as My Spirit of faith imbues them they shall gird up their loins as for battle and know that nothing is impossible to them when it has been spoken by Me. For there are many many, many exploits says the Lord, that My pastors should be doing. But in this past season there has been a great constraining among My pastors, says the Lord. There has been a great constraining and a thwarting of vision and even the struggling to get the sheep to carry the vision forward to any great degree.

But I tell you that in the days to come, the time of stretching and barrenness shall decrease and shall bow its knee to the spirit of faith and revelation which I am about to pour upon My shepherds. And so I shall blow—from the East to the West and from the South to the North—I shall blow across the barrenness with the fierce breath of My Spirit and the constraints and the hindrances shall fall and the negativities shall be demolished. And there shall come the great outpouring of My Spirit of faith and of revelation upon My shepherds. And so it shall be that in a twinkling there shall be an expansion in your Spirit that you shall say: I knew not what to do, but now I know. I knew not how to do, but now I know. I did not have faith to do, but now I do.

AND IT SHALL COME TO PASS IN THAT DAY, THAT THE MOUNTAINS SHALL DROP DOWN NEW WINE, AND THE HILLS SHALL FLOW WITH MILK, AND ALL THE RIVERS OF JUDAH SHALL FLOW WITH WATERS, AND A FOUNTAIN SHALL COME FORTH OF THE HOUSE OF THE LORD, AND SHALL WATER THE VALLEY OF SHITTIM.
JOEL 3:18 KJV

And so it shall be that with the Spirit of faith and of revelation, My pastors shall once again prepare for exploits. And so it shall be that with the Spirit of faith and of revelation, My pastors shall now envision My sheep. And so shall a great shout of rejoicing resound through the lands and the nations as the people join hands and hearts together to build My House. And out of this joining and out of this doing whole communities shall be served and blessed. Whole cities shall be served and blessed. Entire neighbourhoods shall marvel. And so it is that My purposes for My sheep shall be accomplished: the poor shall be fed; the needy shall be clothed; rehabilitation centres shall be built; feeding and evangelistic programmes will be financed; rehousing schemes shall be established; abortion clinics will be closed and My people shall establish places of refuge for My lambs.

But whereas in the past it has been building in the ones and the twos, so shall My Spirit of faith provide a supernatural increase in the ability to do—and so for some it shall be building in the fives and the tens, but for others called apostolically in this hour, it shall be hundreds.

For what you have seen until now, My shepherds, has been but a trickle, has been but a shadow of all that I have stored up for My local churches in the coming season. For as a tap that trickles, so has the measure and the impact of My churches been on your community in comparison to the coming season. For I tell you: Prepare. Prepare for the season of the outpouring. For truly I say to you that where the tap has trickled and there has not been even water to fill a cup, so in this endtime season you shall see across all the nations of the Earth the taps of evangelism and resources turned on. And the waters of living water shall stream and pour forth across communities, across nations, across continents that there will not even be enough room to contain the outpouring as it flows.

Ha! says the Lord. For surely in this age and in this season, My prophets are about to do some strange and some extraordinary things.

Yes, prepare. Prepare yourselves for the extraordinary for I am raising up a people, I am raising up a company of prophets who will act as an abrasion to the body of Christ, for surely there are many of My servants who will even question and wonder at the manner in which My prophets have been called to walk in these days. For I am raising My prophets from the East and from the West, from the South and from the North. And not many are known and not many are well versed. But they are well versed in Me, says the Lord.

For these ones, yes these ones, yes, their faces are set like flint. They will not heed the voice or the system or the politics and manipulations of man or minister. They shall one by one come forth in this time. And they shall not need or require man's favour or reward, for they are a strange and wonderful breed dedicated and holy unto the Lord. For they are neither bribable nor corruptible. For their master is neither mammon nor fame, nor favour. But their master is the mighty Holy One of Israel. And so these ones shall arise, and many many of My ministers shall watch and stand ambivalent. And they shall come forth with a fierce countenance for they do not listen to the voice of man. For they have been trained in the desert place and the wilderness. For they have been raised on misunderstanding and rejections. For they have walked being despised and passed over and have been measured by the judgements of man. And so it is that they now come forth and shine like gold. They can be bought by no man, no ministry, no pastor nor elder.

For they are Mine, says the Lord. As refined by fire, they hold only to Me. They speak only My words. They do only My deeds. And so it is that first one shall rise, and I shall confirm his words with My hand. And then ten shall arise close behind. And then twenty, and then a hundred, and then a thousand, like fire spreading across My Church.

> YEA, AND ALL THE PROPHETS FROM SAMUEL AND THOSE THAT FOLLOW AFTER, AS MANY AS HAVE SPOKEN, HAVE LIKEWISE FORETOLD OF THESE DAYS.
> ACTS 3:24 KJV

And they shall raise their voices in judgement against the false systems of My Church. And they shall raise their hand even as Elijah and My signs and My judgement shall come forth.

And so it is that even My leading ministers shall stand back in wonder and receive these as My prophets for surely the fear and conviction of My Father shall fall upon them and they shall know that these are His, His alone. And so My ministers shall take heed. They shall take account of their ways and so it shall be that because of the fierceness of their rising, so My servants shall fall and shall repent. And so My Church shall turn.

And so because of these mighty unseen ones, I shall stay My judgement. And even as Jonah stayed My hand at Nineveh, so shall My hand be stayed against this disobedient generation of My Church. And so a great outpouring of My mercy shall come forth. Watch well and see this terrible company, for I tell you that even at this hour they rise in your midst. Take care and discern correctly that you may not be found having despised these strange and terrible ones, the prophets of the Most High.

PROPHETIC WORD RECEIVED NOVEMBER 1999

And now in this final hour, it is time for My builders to rise up.

Rise up, rise up, I tell you. Rise up, rise up, you apostles, you called-out ones. For it is time to build My Church. Rise up, rise up, for My House that shall be built by you is a House that shall be of splendour and glory and a wonder to all nations.

Rise up, rise up, My builders for it is your time to arise and to build. And so it is that now I CALL YOU FORTH, AND I CALL NOT MANY OF YOU FROM FINE BUILDINGS BUT I CALL YOU FROM THE ROCKS AND THE CAVES AND THE MOUNTAINS. YOU SHALL COME, for it is in the place of hardness, in the place where you have day by day hewn out stone for My work, from the flinty rock, that you shall come. For I have seen you work as the sun has beaten down on you and I have seen you work as the rain has poured. I have seen you lift up your tools and say: Yes it is hard, yes times are tough but there is work to be done.

And so now I call you forth My sons, now I call you forth. And though your hands have grown calloused with the tools you have used day after day, week after week, through the resistance My sent ones have encountered, surely they have grown strong. And so I say to you this day, that as you have endured in this past   season, as you have persevered, as you have put your back into the hard place—not a place where signs and wonders abound—but a place of day-by-day endurance, so I say to My apostles: It is now your hour.

For I have taught you to build in the hard place without mortar. I have taught you to build without bricks but with straw and with clay. And as you have practised in the rocks and the caves and the mountains, NOW I BRING YOU FORTH into the open field. Now I bring you forth into the temple grounds and so you shall build My House, a House not for man but a House unto Me. A House not of bricks but a House of My people. And your work shall stand, says the Lord. Not just for a day, but for eternity.

For your foundations shall be both sure and strong, says the Lord. You shall build that which is both solid and true, for I have birthed you in strength and in righteousness. I have birthed you in

> YOU ARE BUILT UPON THE FOUNDATION OF THE APOSTLES AND PROPHETS WITH CHRIST JESUS HIMSELF THE CHIEF CORNERSTONE. IN HIM THE WHOLE STRUCTURE IS JOINED (BOUND, WELDED) TOGETHER HARMONIOUSLY, AND IT CONTINUES TO RISE (GROW, INCREASE) INTO A HOLY TEMPLE IN THE LORD (A SANCTUARY DEDICATED, CONSECRATED, AND SACRED TO THE PRESENCE OF THE LORD).
> IN HIM (AND IN FELLOWSHIP WITH ONE ANOTHER) YOU YOURSELVES ALSO ARE BEING BUILT UP (INTO THIS STRUCTURE) WITH THE REST, TO FORM A FIXED ABODE (DWELLING PLACE) OF GOD IN (BY, THROUGH) THE SPIRIT.
> EPHESIANS 2:20-22, THE AMPLIFIED BIBLE

power and in might, that you might do great works for Me. For you have not sought glory for yourself, but surely it is Mine and My glory alone that you have sought. And even in the times when you have been passed by for that which I have placed in My body, that is more spectacular, that seems more appealing, I tell you My child, that now I call you. I call you forth.

Apostles arise. Apostles be doing. Apostles start to build. For whereas in the past the enemy and his hordes have many times dug under the foundations and the building has collapsed, I tell you that in this day, there will be no resistance too strong to those in which I have placed My apostolic call.

For I have placed in them the might of Cyrus and the backbone of Daniel. And so it shall be that as I call them forth, they shall rise. They shall rise in government. They shall rise in the market-place. They shall rise in the media. They shall rise in the palaces. They shall rise among My ministers. They shall rise in the affairs of the Earth and great favour shall be given unto them, great favour. And they shall have the ear of the king and the presidents and the bankers and the pre-eminently wicked who hold great sway in the eyes of mankind. For indeed I tell you that many indeed, many shall sue for their favour.

For until now you have looked for My apostles only in the Church. But I tell you, My Church is far beyond what you think and consider it to be in length, in breadth and in influence. And so it is that many, many of My apostles in this hour shall rise away from the Church structures and shall rise like Joseph and like Daniel, like Moses and like David.

And so from obscurity they shall rise and they shall sit in the Palace and in the White House and in Wall Street. They shall sit in the banks and in computer companies and in governments. They shall sit in Hollywood and in sports arenas and the record companies and the media. For these are indeed the city gates in the endtimes where My elders shall sit. Yes, these are My apostles in this last time, these are My servants. And I will grant them supernatural wisdom and strategies and keys in hidden places that will unlock the nations. So make haste to recognise them, My ministers. Make haste, for they shall build My Kingdom on the Earth and great glory and honour shall rise up to Me from the wicked. For they shall govern with honour and strength and with righteousness.

And so it is now to those who stand in the gap between mercy and judgement, between life and death.

It is to those who I have called and have taught to be well skilled in the secret place, in the place of obscurity, in that place where no man has known your labour and no man has rewarded your tears. And so, it is in this last time that the voice of My Spirit calls out to these, My intercessors: Stand in the gap. Stand in the gap. Stand in the gap between Heaven and Hell. Stand in the gap between mercy and judgement.

For I tell you that in these last days, so My intercessors shall be endowed with the same power and authority with My Father that Abraham had when he pled for the salvation of his people. So My intercessors shall find favour with My Father, if they plead for mercy to triumph over judgement—if they ask My Father to stay His judgement—if only they will plead, if only they will require of Him.

For surely I tell you that even in this season, He sits on His throne weeping for the judgements that have yet to be poured out upon the Earth and upon His beloved Creation. And so He waits. He waits for the ones who will plead for mercy, for the ones who will stand in that place between the living and the dead; and surely I tell you this day, that if His people, beloved of Him, ask Him to stay His hand of judgement, that His hand will be stayed for a

And the Lord said, Because the shriek (of the sins) of Sodom and Gomorrah is great and their sin is exceeding grievous, I will go down now and see whether they have done altogether (as vilely and wickedly) as is the cry of it which has come to Me; and if not, I will know.

Then (Abraham) said to Him, Oh, let not the Lord be angry, and I will speak (again). Suppose (only) thirty shall be found there. And He answered, I will not do it if I find thirty there.

And he said, Oh, let not the Lord be angry, and I will speak again only this once. Suppose ten (righteous people) shall be found there. And (the Lord) said, I will not destroy it for ten's sake.

And the Lord went His way when He had finished speaking with Abraham, and Abraham returned to his place.

Genesis 18: 20-21, 30,32-33 The Amplified Bible

season, that His Creation may look well to their ways.

So lift your voices, beloved. Let your voices ring out to the Father. Let your hands rise high in prayer and supplication to Him. Let your tears fall on behalf of His Creation. And so I tell you, My intercessors, the whole world waits upon your obedience to plead on behalf of a sinful, rebellious and disobedient Creation. And as you plead, so even for one the destiny of mankind shall be. And so I breathe on the North and the South and the East and the West. Intercessors: Come forth. Intercessors: Come forth. I call you in this hour.

I call you in this day. Come into your closets. Come forth to the Father. Come rend your hearts before Him that He may have mercy on those who deserve no mercy, and grace on those who have despised His name and His ways. And then I shall call you forth out of your closets and so in turn you shall go out on the highways and the byways and you shall proclaim the will and the timings of the Lord.

For surely I tell you that in this day, the intercessors shall indeed be imbued by My Spirit and they shall prophesy. They shall prophesy of the things that have been revealed to them in the secret place and I shall send them forth in prayer and supplication. I shall send them onto the streets and into the cities. I shall send them into the bars and the casinos. I shall send them into the dens of the propagators of iniquity and they shall rend their garments. And I shall send them into the high places where idols reign. I shall send them into the high places and they shall pull down the idols and those things that have been an abomination in My Father's sight.

And so for a season My Father's hand of judgement will be stayed. And in that short season so, then beloved, His prophets, that terrible company will rise to meet them, to rise up and to declare His counsel and His warning of impending judgement. And My intercessors shall join with My prophets and become a mighty and fearsome army.

◆TO THE PASTORS, ELDERS AND HOME CELL LEADERS—THE GREAT JOINING AND NEW POWER FOR EVANGELISM ◆

But truly I tell you there is yet another increase about to break forth upon My shepherds.

The Spirit of the Living God cries: EVANGELISM, EVANGELISM.

The Spirit of the Living God cries: SOULS, SOULS.

For there is coming a great spirit of evangelism to be poured out upon My shepherds. There is a new power for evangelism about to be poured out upon My shepherds and upon their elders and upon their leaders and My congregations throughout the Earth. For as My spirit of revelation speaks to them, their hearts will burn within them with divine plannings and with new strategies for evangelism.

And so it is that there will come in this end season a great joining of My shepherds. For in this day and in this hour there shall occur a great joining of My pastors across the cities of the Earth—a great joining across the denominations of the Earth—a great joining across the nations of the Earth.

> AND ALL THAT BELIEVED WERE TOGETHER, AND HAD ALL THINGS COMMON; AND SOLD THEIR POSSESSIONS AND GOODS, AND PARTED THEM TO ALL MEN, AS EVERY MAN HAD NEED.
>
> AND THEY, CONTINUING DAILY WITH ONE ACCORD IN THE TEMPLE, AND BREAKING BREAD FROM HOUSE TO HOUSE, DID EAT THEIR MEAT WITH GLADNESS AND SINGLENESS OF HEART,
>
> PRAISING GOD, AND HAVING FAVOUR WITH ALL THE PEOPLE. AND THE LORD ADDED TO THE CHURCH DAILY SUCH AS SHOULD BE SAVED.
>
> ACTS 2:44-47 KJV

For it is in this day and it is in this hour that the spirit of disunity, the spirit of territorialism, the spirit of competition, the spirit of selfish ambition shall be exposed in the hearts of My Church and so shall rise My true shepherds. They shall come forth with a rod of wisdom and the rod of grace, they shall do all things for My sake and for the sake of My Kingdom. And so shall the witches and the warlocks tremble with the region of the damned. For surely it is the Great Joining they fear—it is the deathblow to the Prince of Division himself.

And so it is that My shepherds and elders shall join with other shepherds and elders across their towns, across their cities, across their nations. And as divine strategy joins with divine strategy— and as My shepherds and elders forgive one another—and lay down their lives one for another—they and their congregations will commit to serve each other and so shall the great joining in the spirit occur. And it shall be a joining of spirit and it shall be a joining of heart. It shall be a joining of finance. It shall be a joining of resources. It shall be a joining of contacts. It shall be a joining of prayer groups. It shall be a joining of congregations.

And as My shepherds join in one accord and pray and seek Me— and as My sheep and My lambs join with one another across neighbourhoods and across city divides and across nations and pray and seek Me—so shall the preparation for the endtime outpouring for evangelism begin.

And so shall My shepherds and their sheep be imbued with power from on high. And I shall mark My sheep with a divine mark that like the Pied Piper will attract the unbeliever wherever they go and Acceleration shall begin. And so shall the division and multiplication of the cell groups greatly accelerate and be the forerunning for the stadium evangelism that shall surely, in the last hours, sweep the cities and nations of the Earth.

And so shall the **witches** and the **warlocks tremble** with the region of the damned. For surely it is the **Great Joining** they fear—it is the **deathblow** to the Prince of Division himself.

For there comes yet a move that is not yet for this hour, says the Spirit of the Living God.

Yes, you shall see a stadium here and a stadium there filled with thousands upon thousands, but that is not My endtime move and it is not the move that My prophets have foretold. For you see, this present season is but the glimmering, it is the outskirts of the endtime move of My Spirit. And anything that you see at this stage of this present Church age, you see but in part. I would say to you: Prepare in these next years. Prepare for all that will come upon you. For it is right and it is good.

But surely I tell you that in the last great outpouring, the stadiums that you see shall be crammed from one city to the next. For I tell you truly that the great outpouring that has yet to even start to manifest upon the Earth will be of such a magnitude that no advertising will be needed. Oh no, says the Spirit of the Living God: No flyers, no banners, no posters, no word of mouth through the saints. For surely I tell you that in the end days as one stadium fills, so too the same weekend stadiums shall be crammed to overflowing in every city across every nation. And it shall be by My sovereign hand, says the Lord God of Hosts.

For in that day, it is not My Church that shall be filling the stadiums. Oh no, for the stadiums shall be filled by the masses of unbelievers. For even as the secular broadcasters come and stare at the nameless faceless miracle workers, so the pre-eminently wicked shall be queuing for hours, even overnight, to get into My arenas, says the Lord.

And so it shall be that as in My days on Earth the sinners were drawn to Me—the Prince of Grace, the lover of the unlovely—so shall My Spirit be manifest to the sinner as it was even when I walked the Earth.

And so as they queue, I shall look upon them and love them. In the arenas all over the nations of the Earth, the sinner shall tremble and cry out, not for fear, but for love of Me. For My Spirit of mercy and compassion to a lost and fatherless generation shall manifest that even some on occasion shall see My hands and face in the clouds above the great stadiums of the world.

once again the Mary Magdalenes of this world shall throw themselves at *My feet*

And so it is that the sinners shall flock once again to hear of My mercy and of My love and of the fearsomeness of My name. And that as in My time—once again the Mary Magdalenes of this world shall throw themselves at My feet and Matthew, the tax collector shall sit with Me and the lepers of HIV shall be cleansed and healed. And those that have stood stout against Me and have even reviled My name on television and through the newspapers of the day shall fall prostrate under My everlasting love and compassions for them.

I, JESUS HAVE SENT MINE ANGEL TO TESTIFY UNTO YOU THESE THINGS IN THE CHURCHES. I AM THE ROOT AND THE OFFSPRING OF DAVID, AND THE BRIGHT AND MORNING STAR. AND THE SPIRIT AND THE BRIDE SAY, COME. AND LET HIM THAT HEARETH SAY, COME. AND LET HIM THAT IS ATHIRST COME. AND WHOSOEVER WILL, LET HIM TAKE THE WATER OF LIFE FREELY.
REVELATION 22:16-17 KJV

And so too the prodigals shall fly in from the four corners of the Earth to sense My presence. And so, I shall manifest Myself finally to the lost sheep of a renegade generation. And the tears shall fall hot and steaming down their cheeks for Me whom they pierced.

And the drug barons shall come—for I love them.

And the pornographic kings shall come—for I love them.

And the fornicators shall come—for I love them.

And the homeless shall come—for I love them.

And the nominal clergy shall come—for I love them.

And the cynics and scoffers shall come—for I love them.

And the bitter and hopeless shall come—for I love them.

And so shall the stadiums be filled with hundreds of thousands of My lost sheep.

And in that day, there shall be no need for any man nor any woman to have an altar call, for the entire arena will be an altar in that day and in that hour. For I, Jesus came to seek and to save that which was lost.

And so it is beloved, that in this present day and this present hour, My ministers see but a shadow of what shall be. And so when you see the stadiums filled with the lost and sinful of the Earth, across the cities of the nations and My presence sweeping the arenas, you shall know that the End is near.

Volume Three

◆ THE CHURCH OF THE LAST AGE ◆

CHRIST MOCKED
MATTHEW 27:29

Volume Three

To the endtime saints whose fervent desire is to be with the Master of Glory—more than to be used by Him.

To the endtime saints who hold His presence and His person dearer than they hold their ministry. To these, His beloved, shall the Lamb indeed entrust the Powers of the Endtime Age of the Church.

The body of Christ must be equipped to persevere and above all be equipped with a mighty fire and flame of the Holy Spirit to suffer in the name of our glorious Lord and Saviour Jesus Christ. To suffer for the preaching and for the proclamation of the Gospel. Yes, we are equipped to build our ambitious Church projects, and yes, we are equipped to believe for our needs and for the needs of the ministry and the needs of others to be met, but I tell you Church: Few of us, if any, are truly equipped in this pallid Western Church for what lies ahead—the persecutions, the sufferings, the martyrdoms—few.

◆

Wherever He is, He is master, when He asks men to make sacrifices, they make them. His call is not that of a fanatic. However, it leads men to deeds of great quality and personal sacrifice.

E.Y. Mullins

Foreword

We have for the past few decades operated in a season of the Church's authority on Earth as the body of Christ. We have used our authority in Christ for healing, prosperity, for dominion and influence as a witness to Christ in this present age, but I tell you dear saint, that the Holy Spirit would prepare us as the body of Christ with a different set of spiritual weapons for what lies ahead, as we enter this last but most glorious age of the Church.

◆

Whereas in the past we have tended to shy away from the subject of suffering, it is now time in the spirit realm where as members of the body of Christ, we must grow up and walk in maturity. It is time to embrace the balance of both God's mercy and God's judgement and that as much as in the past decades we have needed to learn how to walk in the authority of the believer—in faith, in prosperity and in victory—that now in this season, it is the search for the body of Christ to learn to walk equipped to endure.

◆

For I would speak to My body. I would speak to My body: Prepare, prepare for the times that have yet to break upon the Earth.

For up until now, it has been an easy thing to walk in the West as a follower of Mine, says the Lord. And it is only in a few isolated territories across the Earth that My people suffer in My name, that their lives and the lives of their loved ones have truly been laid down for the sake of My Gospel. But I declare to you this day, that a time of suffering draws nigh and is coming soon upon the Earth and I grieve for My Western Church. How I weep for you, My beloved Church, for I tell you, there is none, not one, who is truly equipped for that day that will come upon you.

And I tell you this day: Take heed My Church, take heed for My warning now to you is My mercy. My warning now to you is My grace. Take hold of My mercy, beloved. Take hold of My grace and repent. Change your ways. Embrace My ways. Take little stock in your reputation but take great stock in Mine. Take little stock in your buildings but take great stock in Mine. For My building is My people and you have neglected My people. Yet My children are of infinite value to Me, says the Lord.

Oh My rebuke is indeed My mercy. I am calling My Church to prepare, that she may stand strong to endure and to have the privilege to suffer for My sake and the sake of My Gospel. For up until now many of you, called by Me, have paid the price for your call and you have laboured greatly for your exploits of faith. And it has been well, says the Spirit of God, but now you shall learn to suffer for My Gospel and it is a much higher thing, says the Lord. It is a higher thing to suffer for My Gospel than to do great exploits. Gird up your inner man. Prepare for war, prepare for war. Prepare for a major onslaught in the spirit realm. Gird yourselves up for war, says the Spirit of the Living God. Gird yourselves up, for what starts as satanic onslaughts in the spirit realm will swiftly cross into the realm of the natural. And as you have seen one or two tragedies, I tell you that these shall be as nought compared to what will come. For I tell you that where you now walk in peace and where you walk in freedom of speech, there is yet coming a time, there yet comes a season, where even to speak My name will bring such persecution that many of you—even those who are leaders— will count the cost and not endure.

So you see pastors, you see ministers, I address you, I implore you, prepare yourselves. Prepare your people, prepare your congregations as for war. For they have little endurance, they have not been taught to endure in hardship, they have not been taught to persevere. They have great faith but no endurance. You have taught them to prosper, to eat the finest wheat and build your fine buildings but you have fed them that which is milk, that which will not sustain them in these coming days.

Teach them, teach them, pastor. Teach them, teach them, minister, to suffer hardship for My name's sake. Teach them, teach them, minister. Teach them to endure, teach them to suffer for My name's sake, that they might be of no reputation. For I tell you that as I look across My Church this day, many, many of My people hold their reputation dearer than My reputation. They will not stand in the time to come. Many, many of My people take stock in their possessions, in what they own, in what they possess. They will be found lacking, for I tell you, that there comes a release of wickedness upon the Earth, there comes a time of such darkness upon the Church that all that is temporal shall in a day perish.

AND AT THAT TIME (OF THE END) MICHAEL SHALL ARISE, THE GREAT (ANGELIC) PRINCE WHO DEFENDS AND HAS CHARGE OF YOUR (DANIEL'S) PEOPLE. AND THERE SHALL BE A TIME OF TROUBLE, STRAITNESS, AND DISTRESS SUCH AS NEVER WAS SINCE THERE WAS A NATION TILL THAT TIME. BUT AT THAT TIME YOUR PEOPLE SHALL BE DELIVERED, EVERYONE WHOSE NAME SHALL BE FOUND WRITTEN INTO THE BOOK (OF GOD'S PLAN FOR HIS OWN).
DANIEL 12:1
THE AMPLIFIED BIBLE

And so again My saints shall rise to proclaim My name, for once again they will live for Me alone and My Church shall stand like a flame of fire, like a beacon on a hill that will draw all men unto Me instead of to themselves.

And once again My Church shall be as My first Church where all were as one, where no man possessed but each was a steward, where each day My body gave up their lives dying daily for the sake of My Gospel.

Oh how I weep for how far removed My Church has grown from My true Gospel. Oh how I weep for how far removed My Church is from the message that My sent ones preached. But I tell you that a shaking comes. And once more My Church shall be shaken, she shall be persecuted. Many will count the cost. Some shall even lose their lives for My name's sake.

TAKE LITTLE STOCK IN YOUR BUILDINGS BUT TAKE GREAT STOCK IN *Mine* . . .

And then My glorious Church shall rise. Oh yes THEN shall My glorious Church rise. For surely I came for a Church more glorious than My first Church. I came for a Church where each man and woman and son and daughter laid their life down for the proclamation of My Gospel. Where the cost is counted and embraced that My name might be glorified, that all may be one, that to suffer for My sake is the pearl of great price, that My Gospel may be preached to all nations. That is My glorious Church. That is My spotless Bride, that shall rise at the end of the age.

Oh My Church . . .

. . . Can you not see nor understand, that you walk in but a shadow
of what My Church is ordained to walk in, of what My first Church
walked in? And I hear some of you ministers immediately in your
heart say, 'Yes Lord, we walk in but a shadow. We would do more.
We would see more. We would do great miracles for You.'

And so I would say to you: Until you, until
your congregations, seek Me, Jesus Christ
alone, I tell you, indeed you will not see
greater things. For instead you seek the
miracles. I watch and My heart is torn as
I see My sent ones seek the signs instead of
the sign-giver. They seek My wonders,
yes, they seek My power and My anointing
and I see their congregations follow in
pursuit. And they seek the signs, they seek
the wonders. They seek the anointing.

> BUT IF ONE LOVES GOD
> TRULY (WITH AFFECTIONATE
> REVERENCE, PROMPT
> OBEDIENCE, AND GRATEFUL
> RECOGNITION OF HIS
> BLESSING), HE IS KNOWN BY
> GOD (RECOGNISED AS
> WORTHY OF HIS INTIMACY
> AND LOVE, AND HE IS OWNED
> BY HIM).
> I CORINTHIANS 8:3
> THE AMPLIFIED BIBLE

And so I tell you, My hand is removed from all of these. For in this
dispensation I tell you that My signs and My wonders will only be
given to those who seek Me, not for the power they might receive
or for the anointing they can carry, but because I am their life. I am
their very breath. And so I stretch My hand across the Earth
seeking for a people who would seek My face alone.

Seek My presence for it is to those who love to be with Me—it is to those alone who would seek only Me and not My gifts—it is to these whose lives are laid down for Me, to these beloved ones, I shall pour My Spirit out upon them. I shall pour My Spirit out in these endtimes as I find these ones I trust.

And as I watch them only worship Me—not for My power or My anointing but for the wonder of communing in My presence, then I shall move My mighty hand and I shall pour out a portion of My Spirit upon these precious ones. Not one portion, not two, but manifold. And I shall raise them up and they shall be as flames of fire, and they shall yet speak and utter My Word and My presence shall fall upon the multitudes. And the fire, the fire of My presence shall fall and so shall the multitudes bow down, with their face to the floor. And so shall My power flow, in might, in magnitude, in conviction, in healing power, in miracles.

And this is the great outpouring that shall come from My sovereign hand upon those who truly love Me, upon those beloved ones who seek only My face. For surely they are the ones who hold My person and My presence dearer than their ministry for they want to be with Me more than they want to be used by Me. These are My beloved, these are My trusted ones. And so I shall release them into the four corners of the Earth with passion and with power, with might and with fire.

And they shall light a flame of My Spirit from East to West and from North to South and My healing power shall flow, and miracles of a magnitude hitherto unseen shall manifest and as lightning, so shall My power and anointing manifest in these end days and all the nations of the Earth shall be touched by it. They shall know that I, the Sovereign God, Creator of Heaven and Earth, has visited them, in power, in majesty and in judgement.

For surely they are the ones who hold My person and My presence

dearer than their **ministry**

And so many, many of My children have cried out to Me for the Harvest.

So many of My children have cried out to Me for souls but I declare to you: the Church has yet to shake before the souls of the endtime move will be harvested. Shake, I say to you. Shake, I declare to you. Shake, shake, shake. For there shall be a shaking that shall come upon the endtime Church as it stands today that has never been seen, has never been experienced. And the people shall fall and repent and the pastors and the leaders shall weep and shall wail for the omissions and the failures of My ministers, for they have done those things that they ought not to have done. And they have omitted those things which were required of them. And this they have done in My name.

PUT IN THE SICKLE, FOR THE (VINTAGE) HARVEST IS RIPE; COME, GET DOWN AND TREAD THE GRAPES, FOR THE WINEPRESS IS FULL: THE VATS OVERFLOW, FOR THE WICKEDNESS (OF THE PEOPLES) IS GREAT. MULTITUDES, MULTITUDES IN THE VALLEY OF DECISION! FOR THE DAY OF THE LORD IS NEAR IN THE VALLEY OF DECISION.
JOEL 3:13-14
THE AMPLIFIED BIBLE

But I tell you, there is coming a time when My conviction shall fall across the congregations of the Western Church. There is coming a time when the fear of My Father and the conviction of My Holy Spirit shall fall across My body and My Church shall rend her garments. For she shall see in truth and in purity and she shall repent from her dead works.

For I am calling for a greater degree of holiness in this hour. For I am calling for a greater degree of separation and of holiness and of consecration in this hour. For it shall be that My Church shall in these end days separate from the world. That My Church shall come out of the world and no longer be counted with her, says the Lord.

FOR I AM CALLING FOR A GREATER DEGREE OF SEPARATION AND OF HOLINESS AND OF CONSECRATION *in this hour.*

For too long now, My Father's House has been contaminated by the world. But I have called her to be without spot, without wrinkle and without blemish in this hour. And so I am calling forth My messengers in this hour, says the Lord. I am calling forth My apostles and My prophets. I am calling forth My evangelists and My teachers. I am calling forth My pastors in this hour.

And these called-forth ones shall be My messengers in this hour and they shall cleanse My Bride. They shall prepare My Bride and My messengers shall be like a flame of fire—and as My Word goes forth from them, My apostolic command, My prophetic Word, My instructions, My conviction—so shall My Word descend like an anvil and shall remove the dross from the gold. And so it shall be that even out of the ashes, I tell you that My endtime Bride shall arise, even as from dry bones she will rise—in purity, in holiness, in love, in unity—she will rise, not as individuals, but this rising shall be as one. And My Word shall go out as a flame of fire that shall cover the Earth and this Gospel shall be preached as in a twinkling, says the Lord. The Earth shall be covered with My glory and the glory of My Gospel and it will be done says the Lord, it shall be done. And THEN My Gospel shall be preached to all nations and then shall the end come.

◆ ENDTIME NATIONS ◆

The greatest revivals will come out of the sacrifice of the martyrs

CHINA
and
EAST
ASIA

Beijing ▣

Shanghai ◉

CHINA

Hong Kong ◉

TAIWAN

South
China
Sea

VIETNAM

0   100   200
MILES

PROPHETIC WORD RECEIVED SPRING 2000

CHINA—THE ENDTIME DYNASTY OF THE SON

Oh, for surely I tell you, that even as the sun rises upon the continent of the East, so shall it be that in this time and in this endtime season, so shall it be that the brilliance and the majesty of the Son—the Son of the Living God Himself—shall rise in might and in power and in splendour upon this fortified land.

For even as the Great Wall of China has been marvelled at as one of the seven wonders of this Earth—so says the God of Abraham, Isaac and of Jacob—so too shall men marvel and wonder as they behold the mighty flame of revival and an outpouring of My Spirit hitherto not seen upon the Earth that has yet to sweep across this continent. For even as the Iron Curtain and the Berlin Wall were dismantled in this past season and a great voice of utterance started to arise across Russia, so shall it be as nought compared to what has been ordained and shall be released across the Far East and beyond.

For I tell you, that even as a seal has been set upon China for past millennia—so too it is the coming of Heaven's preordained timings and seasons—and so the great seal of the East shall be broken and a mighty wail of repentance shall resound through the cities and the villages. And a great spirit of supplication and of worship to the Living God and to the Son of God crucified shall arise up to the throne room. And it shall rise to Me not as an incense, not as a fragrance, but it shall rise before My throne fiercely as a living burning flame, says the Living God.

Yes, as a mighty flame the tears and the supplications of My Eastern saints shall rise before Me and it is at this time that the blood of the martyrs and the cries of those imprisoned for My sake and for the sake of My Son and for the sake of this Gospel in China shall be released in the heavenlies. And so it is that a great stirring in the heavens shall occur.

BUT WATCH OUT FOR YOURSELVES, FOR THEY WILL DELIVER YOU UP TO COUNCILS, AND YOU WILL BE BEATEN IN THE SYNAGOGUES. YOU WILL BE BROUGHT BEFORE RULERS AND KINGS FOR MY SAKE AS A TESTIMONY TO THEM.
AND THE GOSPEL MUST FIRST BE PREACHED TO ALL THE NATIONS.
MARK 13: 9-10 WORDS OF JESUS
THE MESSAGE

And so it is that the multitude of the angelic force of the East shall be unleashed, My Holy Warring Angels. And so they shall go forth across the firmaments and set themselves with My saints against the satanic Princes of the East.

And so the seal of the East shall be broken and war shall be declared in the heavens and the flame of My followers—the brilliance of My Son abiding on the inside of My sent ones—shall rise as an inferno, so fierce shall be the brilliance of its rising.

And this flame shall rise across the villages of China and it shall rise into the cities and it shall rise from the farmlands and it shall rise to the government. And it shall rise through the industries and it shall rise even to the heads of state. And as it rises the people shall marvel. And as it rises the West shall marvel. And as it rises, so the great rising of My Son and His Gospel through the East shall cause even kings and queens and presidents to marvel. And so it is that in the heavenlies in this season, this continent shall be called by a new name, the Land of the Rising Son.

And I tell you that in this time and at this season so shall My Spirit be poured forth upon the peoples of the East. And so it is that they shall see Him who was crucified, they shall look upon Him who was pierced for their transgressions, so shall My glory, My conviction and My power, and the fear of My name overshadow this continent.

And so it is that in this time there shall be a brief window of grace for My saints—a window where those imprisoned for My Gospel shall be released—a brief window where My Word will be freely proclaimed among the highways and byways, where even government officials will give their nod to the proclamation of My Gospel across China.

So I warn you My children: Prepare—prepare for this season of grace—for it shall swiftly come upon you in the next years. Prepare, prepare—for where you have been My suffering Church, prepare to be My mass evangelists. For where you have whispered in secret—prepare to shout My Gospel from the rooftops to all of China and beyond. For the Great Wall in the Spirit realm shall crumble and I shall open up a voice of utterance that shall resound into every doorway and every street. A voice of utterance that shall resound in Shanghai. It shall resound in Beijing. It shall resound in Taiwan. It shall resound in Hong Kong. And so the flame of revival shall rise from My believers and shall blaze across China. And this flame of revival shall blaze like a burning bush from the Far East to the Middle East to India—through Western Europe to Eastern Europe—to Africa, Australasia, the Americas even to Vietnam, says the Lord. And the destiny of the endtime Church shall be impacted and repositioned because of the fierceness of the Rising of the Son of the Living God in the Far East. And WHEN all across China have been given an opportunity to hear My Gospel, there is yet a latter season to descend upon China—it shall come swiftly after the season of grace and it shall be a swift deadly silent transition. Yet one day there will be grace and the next there will be death and martyrdom. Yet one day there will be freedom to proclaim the Gospel and the next shall be martial law.

BUT WHEN THEY ARREST YOU AND DELIVER YOU UP, DO NOT WORRY BEFOREHAND OR PREMEDITATE WHAT YOU WILL SPEAK. BUT WHATEVER IS GIVEN YOU IN THAT HOUR, SPEAK THAT; FOR IT IS NOT YOU WHO SPEAKS, BUT THE HOLY SPIRIT.
NOW BROTHER WILL BETRAY BROTHER TO DEATH AND A FATHER HIS CHILD; AND CHILDREN WILL RISE UP AGAINST PARENTS AND CAUSE THEM TO BE PUT TO DEATH.
AND YOU WILL BE HATED BY ALL FOR MY NAME'S SAKE. BUT HE WHO ENDURES TO THE END SHALL BE SAVED.
MARK 13: 11-13
WORDS OF JESUS
THE MESSAGE

Take heed that in the season of grace you do not become lulled to sleep and are found by the enemy to be at ease. For in this latter season a new order of government will seize power and their rule will be a rule of iron and of the Antichrist—a rule of violence, suppression and death.

And so—you will be handed over to death for My name's sake. And so you will be imprisoned and tortured for My name's sake. And even in this present Church age, as you have suffered so much for My Gospel it shall seem, when compared to the violence of this final coming persecution, as nothing. For I tell you that families shall be dragged from their houses and shot in the streets. For I tell you that children shall be shot in squares in front of their parents.

AND SO A

Great Evil

SHALL POSSESS AND OPPRESS CHINA IN PREPARATION FOR

HER RISE TOWARDS ARMAGEDDON WITH THE

KINGS OF THE EAST.

For I tell you crucifixions, beheadings and burnings to death all will be commonplace. And there shall rise once again among the wicked a terrible coldness and a spirit of betrayal which shall even infect the believers. And Christian brother will be handed over to the secret police by Christian brother, and daughter by mother. And so a great evil shall possess and oppress China in preparation for her rise towards Armageddon with the kings of the East.

AND THEY SHALL BE WITH ME AT MY THRONE

in Glory

But those who stand for Me in the face of death and love their lives not even unto death, these are My great beloved whose robes have been dipped in blood. These are the faithful and true. And they shall be with Me at My throne in Glory—My great beloved, My priceless treasure, My own.

Yet one day there will be
grace and the next
there will be death and
martyrdom.
Yet one day there will be freedom to
proclaim
the Gospel and the next shall
be martial law.

The flight into Egypt
Matthew 2:13

THE ARAB NATIONS—VISITATION OF JESUS

How I would weep for you. For as My eyes go back and forth across the Middle East, Oh surely I tell you that in this endtime it is coming your time and your season to hear My Gospel proclaimed.

Oh Syria, Oh Jordan, Oh Persia, Oh Babylon: Prepare yourself. Prepare yourself for a great and mighty visitation of My Spirit. For a great and mighty outpouring of the supernatural is almost upon you. For behold there rises upon the Arab Nations a supernatural visitation of the supernatural and I, the Spirit of Jesus, will find those that hunger and thirst for Me and for My Father and We will manifest Ourselves to them. And so it shall be that you shall hear the report of the Lord from Jordan and from Iran and from Iraq and from Saudi Arabia and from Syria saying: Jesus is appearing to the people. And I tell you that first it shall be one and then two and then ten and then a hundred, and they shall see Him who was pierced for them and they shall throw themselves at My feet and they shall know that it is I that their hearts have sought after, since the beginning of time itself.

And so a great spirit of revelation and visitation shall start to manifest and so a great spirit of supplication and repentance shall sweep the communities for it is I, Jesus, who shall speak. First one behind closed doors, then two behind closed doors, then twenty and then thousands, and so My Church throughout the Arab nations shall start to rise.

And surely even in the United Arab Emirates, I shall appear. And the doors shall be barred. And the curtains shall be drawn but still I shall appear. And I shall appear to the meek and I shall appear to the lowly and I shall appear to the princes and I shall appear to the royal household—for My Church has *still* to rise among the Arab Nations.

And so I am calling Jordan. And I call Egypt. And to you Egypt I commission— you who are ordained to carry My message to your peoples. For I will open doorways for you Egypt to carry My Gospel to the nations and to kings. For I will open doors of utterance through you Egypt to Syria and to Iran. And I will open doors of utterance Egypt through you to Iraq and to Saudi Arabia. For surely Egypt I have called you by name to take My Gospel to your Arab brothers. And I will

NOW AFTER THEY HAD GONE, BEHOLD, AN ANGEL OF THE LORD APPEARED TO JOSEPH IN A DREAM AND SAID, GET UP! (TENDERLY) TAKE UNTO YOU THE YOUNG CHILD AND HIS MOTHER AND FLEE TO EGYPT; AND REMAIN THERE TILL I TELL YOU (OTHERWISE), FOR HEROD INTENDS TO SEARCH FOR THE CHILD IN ORDER TO DESTROY HIM.
AND HAVING RISEN, HE TOOK THE CHILD AND HIS MOTHER BY NIGHT AND WITHDREW TO EGYPT.
MATTHEW 2:13-15
THE AMPLIFIED BIBLE

place upon you a mighty portion of My Spirit—upon your believers. And as they go, I will grant them favour to speak where none have spoken and to proclaim what has never been proclaimed. And I will open the way for My Gospel to be proclaimed throughout the Arab Emirates, through Egypt, says the Lord. For even as you, Egypt, were once a protection for Me when I was a babe fleeing from Herod's grasp—so once again, you shall be the Father's instrument to protect the Christ and His Gospel in this time. And so too with you will come Jordan, and so Lebanon and Syria—yes even Syria—is yours for the taking, says the Lord. For surely I am the One who sets kings and governments in office and I am the One who tears down.

And so it is that there shall come a softenening, even in the high places of the Arab Emirates. And it shall be an underground outpouring, and the whisper shall rise in the streets and behind closed doors and a great rush of My Spirit shall roar and My Gospel shall yet be proclaimed.

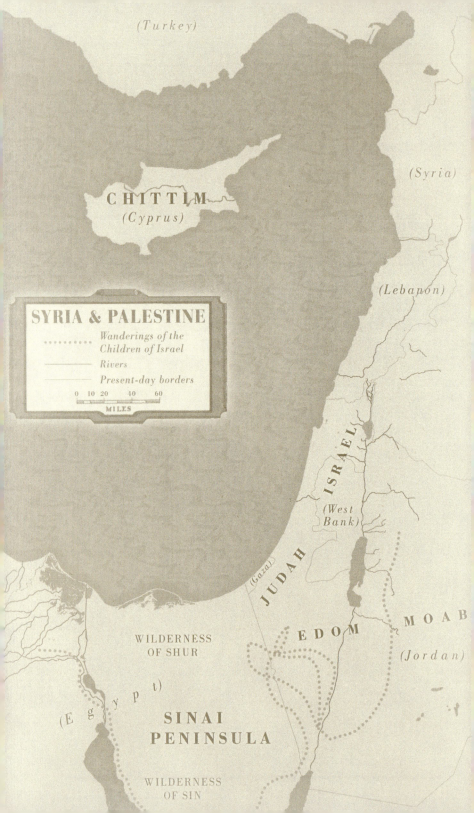

(Turkey)

CHITTIM
(Cyprus)

(Syria)

(Lebanon)

SYRIA & PALESTINE

············· *Wanderings of the*
           Children of Israel
——————— *Rivers*
——————— *Present-day borders*

0 10 20   40   60
—————————————————
MILES

ISRAEL
(West Bank)

(Gaza)

JUDAH

WILDERNESS
OF SHUR

EDOM

MOAB

(Jordan)

(E g y p t)

SINAI
PENINSULA

WILDERNESS
OF SIN

ISRAEL—INTRODUCTION

And so now we come to the subject that is so close to the Father's heart and has therefore unleashed such satanic rage throughout history—that even this past generation, one of the most shocking events to stand out in twentieth-century history was that of the Holocaust, where in the midst of civilised European society, over six million Jews were murdered, incinerated or died in concentration camps. But as controversial as Israel is to a sector—and as much as even its whisper causes the hellish regions of the Earth to erupt in satanic rage—it simply cannot be disputed biblically that God the Father Himself—the God who named Himself out of every nation of the Earth as the God of Israel and who chose His only begotten Son to be birthed of a Jewish Virgin girl in Nazareth, Israel—has declared a covenant with the Jewish people, which today still stands as steadfast and binding in Heaven as when the Father first declared it with Abraham, whom He declared: FRIEND OF GOD.

> AND I WILL ESTABLISH MY COVENANT BETWEEN ME AND THEE AND THY SEED AFTER THEE IN THEIR GENERATIONS FOR AN EVERLASTING COVENANT, TO BE A GOD UNTO THEE, AND TO THY SEED AFTER THEE.
> GENESIS 17:7 KJV

I have an overwhelming conviction—I believe by the Spirit of the Living God Himself that the Father's focus on Israel as we start to enter the beginning hours of the Church's endtime season, is not only undiminished, but I believe has and will now continue to intensify with each passing year. As it was in the days of the Father's covenant with Abraham, Lucifer's railing and rage knew no bounds so it was prophesied that the seed that would bruise his heel would come forth from the Jewish nation. And after that last moment of Golgotha, as Jesus Christ descended into hell, a great wail arose from the bowels of hell hissing: 'Destroy DESTROY . . . Destroy the Jewish people. Destroy the Father's beloved. Destroy those from whom my arch-enemy Messiah was born. Destroy every Jew.'

And so through the ages we have seen, in ever-increasing measure, his violent satanic fury once more released to outwork its way upon the Earth through disobedient sons of man. This past generation saw six million of God's covenant people perish with the Church of Jesus Christ standing by as an uneasy ashamed silent witness.

But today—as we enter the end days—we are faced with a wake-up call. The Father, who Himself is named the God of Israel, the God of Abraham, Isaac and Jacob, would call out His true Church to raise up their voice on behalf of a people—maybe stiff-necked and rebellious—but who have been sovereignly chosen and ordained as His beloved. I have an overwhelming conviction that this is not, in this endtime, merely an option but is a direct command of the Father, the Jewish God and His Son, born a Jew.

How desperately He must have grieved in the 1940s while apart from His few heroic servants like Dietrich Bonhoeffer, the majority of His people sat in congregations all around Europe, America, Canada and the Western world praising His name and yet were either completely disinterested in the fate of the Jewish people or not prepared to identify with them because of the possible consequences . . . It can never occur again.

We will in these next few decades be given another chance, as the true Church of Jesus Christ, to stand with Israel and our Jewish brothers and sisters against the violent unbridled rage of Lucifer Himself manifested in a more vicious and far spreading wave of anti-semitism than even the Holocaust.

Still today there are occasions when the nominal church label the Jews 'Christ haters' because the Jewish people crucified Jesus. But what the world often forgets is that the first Jewish disciples, Peter, James and John—whom Jesus loved—and Stephen, who laid down his life, were the first most passionate Christ lovers. Oh, how the Father loves His Jews.

Where will you stand, beloved brother and sister? For truly I tell you, that to disregard the cause of Israel and her people is to disregard the cause of the Most Holy Father Himself.

I HAVE AN OVERWHELMING CONVICTION THAT THIS IS NOT, IN
THIS ENDTIME,
MERELY AN OPTION
BUT IS A DIRECT
COMMAND OF THE FATHER,
THE JEWISH GOD AND HIS SON,
BORN A *Jew*

ISRAEL—MY BELOVED—THE FATHER SPEAKS

Oh, for surely I tell you beloved, even now this day, Jerusalem—that your walls are ever before Me. And even now I would still gather you into My arms as a hen gathers her chicks. But you would not. But still I weep for you, My beloved Israel. For My covenant of love and commitment to you shall never be broken but shall continue from generation to generation. Oh, for was it not you I chose out of all the peoples of the Earth and yes, I covenanted to you and drew you unto Me, My beloved. For was it not out of you that came My prophets and was it not out of you that My own beloved, only begotten Son came forth?

Oh yes Israel—and so it was that even as you crucified My Son, still I loved you. Even as through the centuries you rejected Me through your blindness, still I loved you. And so it was that even in the midst of the turmoil and grieving of the Holocaust, so My sovereign hand rested upon you. And so it was that I brought you out of the devastation and the abandonment by both enemies and friends until your voice once again as a remnant cried out to Me through the heavens.

And so it was by My mighty arm as with Moses of old, so I brought you, My people, and I gathered you together. That even as the nations of the world once again behind closed doors marshalled their voices together against you so I sent My mighty warring angels forth and Michael himself fought against the satanic princes on your behalf. And as in the days of old, I brought you back with great joy and rejoicing to your land and My land, the land of Israel.

And even as the world looked upon the small and pitiful state and once again mocked, so too through the decades My sovereign hand has been upon you to prosper you, to bless you, to water you, to protect you. And how could it be—were it not for the hand of the Living God—that such a remnant could bring the world to a standstill?

Oh, for surely I have made it known that when Israel wars—the nations gather—even the Western and the Arab nations and the Eastern nations' eyes are upon Israel because My eye is upon Israel. And so beloved, in the same manner that you have seen My mighty outstretched hand in the years of war gone by, so you shall see My mighty outstretched hand in the years to come. For many are your enemies, Oh Israel and even those that speak peace to you, speak with forked tongues. For many shall come to you to sue for favour but they shall come with forked tongue.

And so, I would speak to you Israel, Oh Israel, My beloved—to gird up your loins—gird up your loins as for war. For you will be as one who lives as in peace but who is always equipped for war. For in the future years the nations shall start to assemble around you as around a prey that is good for food. And even though they talk peace, their hearts are far from peace and there is no truth in them.

And it is in this time, Oh Israel, that as the rumours and the sounds of war grow stronger—that once again you shall come up and enquire of Me. And the man in the street shall enquire of Me—and the soldiers shall enquire of Me—and the learned scholars shall enquire of Me—and even those in the government and in the hidden high places shall once again enquire of Me.

Oh, and as you enquire of Me, so My heart rejoices and I shall hear your supplications. And I shall give ear to your prayer. And so it is that in these coming end days, when the times of the Gentiles is complete, so shall I with My sovereign mighty hand, move My arm as the God of Israel, the Holy One once again in your midst. And so it is in this day and in this hour, that as you seek Me—and as you enquire of Me—and you seek Me with all your heart—as one nation—you shall see Him that thou pierced. Every eye shall see Him, every ear shall hear Him.

AND WHAT ONE NATION IN THE EARTH IS LIKE THY PEOPLE, EVEN LIKE ISRAEL, WHOM GOD WENT TO REDEEM FOR A PEOPLE TO HIMSELF, AND TO MAKE HIM A NAME, AND TO DO FOR YOU GREAT THINGS AND TERRIBLE, FOR THY LAND, BEFORE THY PEOPLE, WHICH THOU REDEEMEDST TO THEE FROM EGYPT, FROM THE NATIONS AND THEIR GODS? FOR THOU HAST CONFIRMED TO THYSELF THY PEOPLE ISRAEL TO BE A PEOPLE UNTO THEE FOR EVER: AND THOU, LORD, ART BECOME THEIR GOD.

2 SAMUEL 7:23-24 KJV

And so it is that a great spirit of mourning and supplication shall sweep through Jerusalem and through Israel as My people gaze on Him whom they pierced. And as My people gaze upon My beloved Son, so shall she rend her garments. For they shall look upon His glorious face, the fairest of ten thousand. And so it is that they will stand amazed: For He is one of us, they will say. And so indeed, Jesus Himself shall gather them to His bosom. And finally, Jerusalem shall be comforted in the arms of her Messiah.

TO GERMANY

Oh, and so it is to My servants, to My children who love and serve Me in the German nations that I would speak. For even now there are those that I am raising up to take up the cause and the standard of My people Israel. For there is a divine marking in the spirit realm upon Germany and the surrounding nations that in the latter days My servants shall rise up around Israel and the Jewish people and shall stand as a covering and as a protection with faces set like flint.

For even before the Holocaust, I saw this day. For even before the Holocaust, I had given Germany a divine endtime mandate to stand side by side with Israel My people. And so it was that the devil himself sought to thwart My endtime plan and use the very nation and vehicle that was intended to raise up and protect Israel to destroy them.

> AND I WILL BLESS THEM THAT BLESS THEE, AND CURSE HIM THAT CURSETH THEE: AND IN THEE SHALL ALL FAMILIES OF THE EARTH BE BLESSED.
> GENESIS 12:3 KJV

But this day, I declare to you, Germany, that your days of guilt and restitution are completed. And the Lord God of Israel would speak to you: Germany, RISE UP, RISE UP, RISE UP. Rise up Church. Rise up, the Church of Jesus Christ. Rise up. For I have lit a burning fire in you Germany. For out of your ashes shall rise flames of fire. For out of you shall rise a fervent roar, the roar of Jesus Christ. And the same way that you marshalled behind Hitler, so shall you marshall behind Jesus Christ and His cause.

And so the Church in Germany shall start to burn. And its flame shall be strong and pure and clear and without guile. And it shall light Europe. And it shall blaze across Africa. And it shall PROTECT Israel. It shall PROTECT Israel.

ISRAEL—BETRAYAL BY HER ALLIES

For surely I tell you that this is a time of transition—a time when voices say: Peace, peace where there is no peace, says the Lord. And even those nations that had previously come to your aid Israel, shall betray you. For there hastens a season and a day when I shall allow the thoughts and motives and intents of the nations and governments to resurrect to the surface that you may be in no doubt as to who is your friend and who is your enemy.

For until now, even over the last years—many, many have whispered peace to you and have even sued for your favour, but it was in their interest and to their advantage. But in the next season, and in this next day, you shall see a great falling away of those around you who until now have stood the middle ground, says the Lord God of Hosts. For even the governments of the West and the Western Powers shall shift and sway and even those who you thought were solid allies to you—shall in the coming days shift allegiance.

For you see, My Spirit has heard the conversations in the corridors of the White House and I have heard the conversations in the high secret places of the Earth. For I have heard the whispered conversations of the bankers and the traders of oil and the armaments of the Earth. For My Spirit has been there among the dark places of mankind. And I tell you: Their words rise up like a stench in My nostrils against My people, Israel. For each is a betrayer, for each one is full of treachery, each one looks to that which is expedient. For you dwell among enemies, Oh Israel, even your named few friends are your enemies. There is not one, no, not one among the nations and the traders of the Earth that is true. And I am grieved with a great grieving.

So, it is now in this season that even your hidden enemies shall arise and yes, it shall seem as even on one day that the whole world has forsaken you. But know this, Oh Israel: they may forsake you, but I will never forsake you—they may desert you, but I, the Lord your God, the Holy One of Israel will never forsake you. No, never so. When the veil starts to be lifted from those who profess to be your friends, and your allies start to scatter to the uttermost parts of the Earth—so in that moment you shall hear the sounds of war and the sounds of war shall increase. Yes and in the twinkling of an eye, so shall they unite against you. And you shall say: We are without help. We shall be driven into the sea. But I tell you that in that day and in that hour you shall call upon My Name and I Myself shall sovereignly scatter them.

I shall winnow them and I shall make you a terror among the nations. And they shall shake because of My sovereign hand upon you. And they shall scatter in terror because of their terror at the might of your God. And so shall Michael, mighty Prince of Israel and his mighty angelic warriors, join with you and a great victory shall occur. And then there shall be peace for a season, until the time of the great end when all nations shall gather against thee— from the East and the West and the South and the North—at that battle called Armageddon.

Keep not thou silence, O God: hold not thy peace, and be not still, O God. For, lo, thine enemies make a tumult: and they that hate thee have lifted up the head.

They have taken crafty counsel against thy people, and consulted against thy hidden ones.

They have said, Come, and let us cut them off from being a nation; that the name of Israel may be no more in remembrance. For they have consulted together with one consent: they are confederate against thee:

The tabernacles of Edom, and the Ishmaelites; of Moab, and the Hagarenes; Gebal, and Ammon, and Amalek; the Philistines with the inhabitants of Tyre; Assur also is joined with them: they have holpen the children of Lot. Selah.

Psalm 83:1-8 KJV

Volume Four

◆ JUDGEMENT ◆

MOSES BREAKING THE TABLETS OF THE LAW
EXODUS 32:19

Volume Four

To the leaders, the ministers and the congregations
of the Western Church in this final dispensation.

The warning of impending judgement is indeed the
Sovereign God's mercy and grace in this last hour.
Take heed, minister of the Gospel.
Take heed, apostle, prophet, evangelist.
But especially to you pastor, and to you teacher,
take heed. For unto you has been given
great accountability in this past season. Do
not be found wanting.

◆

THE SAGES AND HEROES OF HISTORY ARE RECEDING
FROM US, AND HISTORY CONTRACTS THE RECORD OF
THEIR DEEDS INTO A NARROWER AND NARROWER PAGE.
BUT TIME HAS NO POWER OVER THE NAME AND DEEDS
AND WORDS OF JESUS CHRIST.

WILLIAM E. CHANNING

Foreword

I have been almost overshadowed by the Spirit of God to write these warnings to a jaded and overfed generation of pastors and ministers in the Western Church in this age. We enter a dispensation where the true prophetic will bring about both mercy in one hand and judgement in the other. But I have to warn you, my brother and sister, His judgement rises upon His leaders, upon those who have been placed in positions of power, influence and responsibility.

◆

Some are ordained by God, many, however, are there by their own hand, by manipulation, by unsanctified ambition.

◆

It is to you, minister of the Gospel, you who are pastors, teachers, evangelists, apostles and prophets, that these words hold a sterner warning. For as much revelation as you have been given, how much more, servant of God, will you be held accountable. For the day of the Lord draws near and He would, in this time, mete out mercy and the comfort of His Spirit to His little ones, to His sheep rejected and cast aside by the body, we term the Church today. But to His ministers, the grace is not in this dispensation granted so freely. For surely it is a time of reckoning, a time of examination, a time to take stock, a time of account as He prepares to rain judgement on His Church.

I warn you, ministers of the Gospel, turn away from your works, works that build your kingdom, works that glorify not the Master but the empires you cling to so avidly. Turn away from the approvals of men around you, the prosperity and the trappings that you voice to be for the Kingdom but are merely to serve your own ends.

Cleanse yourselves, you who proclaim His Word. Look to your own house and see if it is not in ruins. For the Lord is grieved with the hypocrisy of His own. For the Lord is grieved at His servants who minister for Him from the pulpits of the day, from the television screen and from the platforms of the world stage. For His ministers have allowed themselves to reign as idols in men's hearts. For His ministers have drawn men and women to themselves and have neglected to point them to His Son, the glorious One we serve.

. . . WHO IMAGINE THAT GODLINESS OR RIGHTEOUSNESS IS A SOURCE OF PROFIT (A MONEY-MAKING BUSINESS, A MEANS OF LIVELIHOOD). FROM SUCH WITHDRAW.
I TIMOTHY 6:5
THE AMPLIFIED BIBLE

Take heed, minister of the Gospel, you whose security rests with your database, your monthly letters, your fund-raising schemes and not with the Lord of Hosts. For the Lord will shake and examine your motives. Let your hands and heart be found pure in this coming day, that you may not be found wanting.

Take heed to yourselves, you pastors, for so much authority has been given you this past generation, yet many have ignored His sheep and fawned upon those in their congregations with power and sway—those with charisma and influence—leaving the poor and oppressed defenceless and ignored. You would indeed do well to examine yourself pastor, for the Spirit of God issues a warning to the pastors, the pastors who have looked to their own needs, who have served their own first while His House is left in ruins. For He does not put stock in your aggressive building plans while His people are left weak, despised, oppressed and passed over in your congregations. For His people are His building and the cries of His people have risen up to Him.

Take heed, minister of God. Take heed for I tell you, we enter a time when the judgement of Jehovah Himself will fall. Let your hands and heart be found pure in this coming day that you may not be found wanting.

THE BUYERS AND SELLERS DRIVEN OUT OF THE TEMPLE
LUKE 19:46

Tell My Church, tell My Church that I weep for them.

Tell My Church that My heart grieves, that I watch as they go about My business, that I watch as they buy and sell, all in the name of My beloved Father. That I watch as they turn His House into a mockery, into a market-place. Ask My leaders, ask My ministers, ask the ones whose livelihood is based on the buying and the selling of the trade in My Father's House, if there is not one of them that discerns? Is there not one that divides rightly?

Do they not yet comprehend that My Father is My very breath, the great King of eternity, incorruptible, invisible, the only true God? And so My heart breaks as I see the desecration of My Father's name as My Own body join Him to the spirit of the world. I watch as My Own turn My Father's House into a market-place and all that is done—the buying and the selling, the trading—is all done in His glorious name, in the name of My Father.

And I tell you this day, that My heart has been stirred and now I am rising in judgement against those who call Me, who call My Father their own, to herald in judgement. Oh open your ears, My Church, open your ears and repent, for no longer will My Father's name be made a mockery. No longer will My Father's House be a house of trade.

And yet I hear you say, 'No, not me, Lord. Not My ministry.

We serve You, we minister for You.'

And I would say to you: Take heed, minister of the Gospel and check your deeds. Look well to that ministry that has been entrusted to you. For indeed I tell you, that even you have been found wanting in the scales and balances of your ministerial affairs. For I tell you what you term 'righteous weights' are wanting by the standards of Heaven. What you call 'ministry business' is called whoredoms in the standards of Heaven. Look well to yourselves, ministers of the Gospel, those who condone the system and the strategy for the end result to proclaim My Gospel. The system and the strategies rise like a stench in My Father's nostrils. The controls, the bribes, the commissions, the manipulations, the politics that rise from My Father's House.

Take heed, minister of the Gospel and look well to your affairs, for too often your ministerial kingdoms, your ministerial empires have been built on the violence of unsanctified ambition, on bribery and treachery, all done in the name of My Father. For I have seen you as you draw men, not unto Me, not unto My Father, but money and strategy is poured into drawing men unto yourselves and unto your ambitions.

And I would ask you this day: How is it that you have strayed so far from My Father's Gospel? How is it that you are so far removed? For each looks to his own kingdom. Each looks to his own house. Everyone looks to his own advantage. And yet as everyone looks to his own, so they proclaim it to be not their own

but to be that of My Father. But I tell you this day that My Father's House has become a mockery, for it has become splintered and fragmented into men's own kingdoms. Kingdoms that do not serve the glorious One—the Creator of Heaven and Earth—but kingdoms that serve mammon, kingdoms that serve man and men's own ministries, their own churches,
their own territories.

Oh how I have watched as pastor has fought against pastor. Oh how I have grieved as ministry has competed against ministry for position, for influence, for men's esteem, and these works are done in the name of My Father.

AND HE WENT INTO THE TEMPLE, AND BEGAN TO CAST OUT THEM THAT SOLD THEREIN, AND THEM THAT BOUGHT; SAYING UNTO THEM, IT IS WRITTEN, MY HOUSE IS THE HOUSE OF PRAYER: BUT YE HAVE MADE IT A DEN OF THIEVES.
LUKE 19:45-46 KJV

But I tell you, these works are not My Father's works, for these motives are not My Father's motives and these ends are not My Father's ends. For I hear your conversations. Your conversations rise up to the throne room of Heaven and I tell you that brother in Christ rises against brother in Christ, sister in Christ, against sister, father against son. All belong to My Father's family. All are sons and daughters of My Father's House. Their tongues are like vipers' tongues. There is no truth in them.

And so I tell you that the time draws near when judgement will come to My own, to purge, to cleanse, to prune that which does not bear fruit. And I tell you beloved, that as I judge, I weep for My House. For My House has strayed so far from that which is pure and which is righteous in My Father's sight. And so today I tell you that My judgement is My mercy to My Father's House. That My discipline, My chastening, is My grace to My Father's House. For I am calling out a people unstained by the spirit of the world. I am calling out a people pure and blameless. I am calling out a people called solely unto the Father and Me.

For We search for a people that We can dwell with. For We search out a people in whom We can make Our abode, that they might be Our very dwelling place. For We search across the Earth in this day for those who cry out for Our very person and for Our very presence and it is to these in this last time, it is to these who love the Father and who abide with the Son and who walk hand in hand with Our Spirit, surely it is to these that We shall reveal Ourselves. Take heed My son. Take heed My daughter and look to your ways.

Woe to you, shepherds who have not fed My sheep.

I speak woe to you pastors who have not fed My sheep. I say woe to you, pastors of the Western Church who have not fed My sheep but who have fed on the gold and silver. Who have decked yourselves in finery and bedecked yourself with jewels, but not from My hand, says the Lord. For I am about to take out of your hand, congregations. I am about to take out of your hands, your influence. I am about to take from your hand, wealth and prosperity.

And you shall know that it is, I, the Lord your God, who have done this thing. And I have done it because you looked to your own regard rather than My people. I have done it because you have served yourselves and your families and your elders rather than serving My people. And so I will remove from you your influence and I shall grant My people shepherds who will feed them, shepherds who will bind up their broken hearts, shepherds who will spend themselves for those who lack, who will feed the poor, who will comfort the grieving, who will deliver the oppressed.

For these ones will be My pastors. For in this day of the Lord that approaches, in this day, I will raise up the faithful and many will arise from obscurity. Many will rise from the shadows. For until now they have been unseen but these are My faithful ones, these are My proven ones. These are the ones whose heart is My heart.

Son of man, prophesy against the shepherds of Israel; prophesy and say to them, even to the (spiritual) shepherds, thus says the Lord God: Woe to the (spiritual) shepherds of Israel who feed themselves! Should not the shepherds feed the sheep? You eat the fat, you clothe yourselves with the wool, you kill the fatlings, but you do not feed the sheep. The diseased and weak you have not strengthened, the sick you have not healed, the hurt and crippled you have not bandaged, those gone astray you have not brought back, the lost you have not sought to find, but with force and hard-hearted harshness you have ruled them. Thus says the Lord God: Behold, I am against the shepherds, and I will require My sheep at their hand and cause them to cease feeding the sheep, neither shall the shepherds feed themselves any more.

Exekiel 34:2-4, 10
The Amplified Bible

And so My sheep will no longer be scattered as without shepherds but in this last time I will grant My people shepherds after My own heart, shepherds that shall lay down their own life for that of My sheep. Shepherds who are not hirelings but are servants. Shepherds who look to the needs of My flock rather than to the needs of themselves and their own.

For the cries of the oppressed, and the cries of the suffering in the congregations have risen up to Me. Even as My people's cries rose up to Me when My people were oppressed in Egypt. And so in the same way that I raised up a deliverer from among them, that I raised up Moses, so at this time My eyes search to and fro across the whole Earth as I weigh and consider the hearts of My shepherds. And to those who have faithfully tended My flock, to those who have put their needs second and who have placed the needs of the suffering, the wounded, the oppressed and the poor above their own needs, it is to these that I shall raise up in this time to care for My sheep.

For I tell you that I search for My shepherds. I seek them out. Many have been hidden and are unseen from view. But to that remnant that even now in this time have been found faithful, these are the ones that I shall multiply. I shall multiply them upon the hills and the valleys. I shall multiply them over the cities and nations and My people shall find under their rod, a rod not of iron, but a golden sceptre, a rod of mercy, a rod of wisdom, a rod of grace. And so indeed, these are the ones who shall train My disciples. These are the ones I have found faithful and these are the ones to whom much shall be entrusted in this last hour.

And now to My generals.

For there are still some of these, some of you generals who have been faithful to Me and although I have grieved at the systems you use, My heart of compassion has seen those who have abused you. And therefore in this time of transition, I have allowed you this grace to use so that you could protect yourself. But it is not My best, My child, for although you are called to be a general, you are first and foremost still My child.

Listen closely now, My child, for so often you still call upon Me as a general and not as My child. And now that will change for you see, yes—I have given you influence—I have granted you authority and influence with people of the Earth. But beloved, being called to be a general has never given you the right to decide, for it has led often to pride, even in your own ministry.

And this day I call you with compassion, Oh beloved child. Yes I have seen you suffer for My sake, for My Gospel's sake and I hold it as a pearl of great price, in those lonely times, times when others have no inkling of the pressures and the strains of a world commission. But My child, I have also grieved as I have seen you suffer for your own mistakes, for you did not come to Me. I have seen you suffer at times not for My Gospel but for the sake of your own work, for your own ambitions and the ambitions of those around you.

But I will never make your ambitions My ambitions, for the one is hay and stubble and the other is fine gold. For at times, beloved, your great plans for the work of the ministry—they are your plans and purposes—but they are not of Me. And when you birth that which is not of Me, it will become a burden in the years to come and greatly will you suffer for that.

For you see, beloved sons and daughters called in this time for Me, you now enter a season where all that is birthed apart from Me will not prosper, where all plans and strategies purposed in your own heart will not prosper. And so today I am calling you, calling you out of your works, out of your plans. For I have granted you great influence, but you must walk in humility and realise—yes, understand My child—that just because you have the power, the wealth, the influence to DO, does not mean by any means at all, that I condone what you purpose to do which rises from your own mind, your own ambitions and your own desires.

You now enter a season where no longer can you tread lightly in the decisions that you make, for those very same decisions that you make, as you have so glibly and lightly in the past. For indeed, I have seen you, even with your boards dismiss certain plans as irrelevant, when My hand has been upon them. And I have seen you embrace that which suits your purpose and the purpose of those around you, but has not been My purpose, nor the purpose of My Father.

For as you live for but a short season here—and you build for here—the Father and I build for eternity. We build for Our Church and much of what has been built in My Father's name will be burnt in a twinkling before My Father's judgement. Build wisely My child, for these decisions that are entered into lightly, without the blessing of My Father, will indeed be the very stumbling blocks that the evil one would raise up against you in this next season.

Be warned beloved, do nothing apart from Me. Do nothing apart from My instruction to you. For whereas in past seasons My grace has been available to cover your weaknesses and to cover your mistakes, My grace is now lifting from My leaders and their compromises as My Church enters this final phase of her life on Earth.

Be warned beloved. Take heed and build My Church wisely. Take heed and place men around you who speak My Words and hear My voice. For many of you still surround yourselves with those who flatter and those who prophesy lies in My name. Many of you still surround yourselves with those equipped to run secular ventures, who are called to run an industry not My ministry.

> FOR WE PREACH NOT OURSELVES, BUT CHRIST JESUS THE LORD;
> AND OURSELVES YOUR SERVANTS FOR JESUS' SAKE.
> 2 CORINTHIANS 4:5 KJV

Look well to those around you. Look well to whose advice and to whose counsel you take heed of. For surely in the years to come, all those who are led by the systems and the manipulations of the world shall lead the ministry I have entrusted to you out of the will of My Father and each shall follow his own way.

Take heed, man of God, take heed as to what you hear. Draw counsel from He who is wisdom. Draw counsel from those who walk with Me as wisdom, and surely your ways, and surely the works of your hands shall prosper greatly. Do not let the machine that has been birthed from your call dictate your direction. Walk with Me as wisdom and as wisdom I shall indeed direct your path.

For My anger has been stirred, yes, says the Spirit of God. Surely My anger has been stirred.

For I have seen My handmaidens, My ministers, the wives of My leaders, the wives of My elders, those men and women who sit in the congregations of the Earth. Their conversations have risen up to Me. Their conversations have risen like a stench in My Father's nostrils and now I call them to account. For no longer will I tolerate this in My congregations, nor in My body. For I have watched silently as you have criticised My people as you have judged. But your judgements have been short-sighted and they have been shallow judgements, says the Lord. And now those very judgements shall rise up once again in judgement against thee.

For you have been unfaithful with that which I entrusted to you. For I waited for mercy and compassion and understanding to arise in you. I waited for you to bind up My broken-hearted in your congregations—for you to reach out your hand of compassion to the oppressed—for you to have mercy upon those upon whom I would mete mercy. But none of these you have done.

For I have seen you and those around you—those you have influenced in this way—point the finger at those you consider lowly. I have seen you scoff and revile in your heart at those you consider weak. I have heard you converse disparagingly about those you consider meek and of no repute. For they did not have the wealth and the influence and the standing that you held as dear. But I tell you, you men and women of idle words, that I am about to wrest the designer Church from your grasp. For surely you have proved yourself unfaithful. For even though your ways and thoughts are cleverly disguised, your measures are the measures of man.

For I see your measures, and the measures of those around you, are the measures of the spirit of the world. They are the measures of the pride of life, of materialism and status in your communities, even your measures are measures of spiritual stature and influence. I have seen you speak with a crooked tongue, for you speak one thing to My children and then behind their back you erode their reputation. I see you feed on idle gossip and propagate it, in the name of prayer. I see you flatter and then I watch you despise in your heart the hurting, the oppressed, the broken-hearted and the struggling.

And now I come to you and I declare to you, that even as the whitewashed sepulchres of My time on Earth, you are all clothed in prosperity and perfectly groomed but your heart has become jaded and your mouth speaks not truth. And so I would say to you this day, My son, My daughter, come before Me and rend your garments. Come down from that pedestal and repent before Me that I may grant you a heart of flesh for your heart of stone.

For I seek for women of compassion in this day. Surely I seek for My sons and daughters who hold My heart, a heart of mercy for the oppressed, a heart of compassion for the meek and lowly. I seek for those whose tongues are purified by fire. I seek for those of My sons and daughters who will spend their life to feed My poor. For those who will minister from a spirit of love and compassion to feed the poor in spirit. For those who will bind up the broken-hearted.

IF INDEED YOU (REALLY) FULFIL THE ROYAL LAW IN ACCORDANCE WITH THE SCRIPTURE, YOU SHALL LOVE YOUR NEIGHBOUR AS (YOU LOVE) YOURSELF, YOU DO WELL. BUT IF YOU SHOW SERVILE REGARD, (PREJUDICE, FAVOURITISM) FOR PEOPLE, YOU COMMIT SIN AND ARE REBUKED AND CONVICTED BY THE LAW AS VIOLATORS AND OFFENDERS.
JAMES 2:8-9
THE AMPLIFIED BIBLE

For your measures are not My measures. For the evil one has sought to hold the whole world in his grasp as the measure of a woman is in her appearance and the measure of a man is in his status. But I tell you that the measure of My sons and My daughters is upon the motive and intent of their heart. For indeed the very men and women that I am about to raise in this the last hour, they are the ones who have been abused, of no repute. They are My despised ones. Ones who have little status in the world's eyes.

But I tell you, that in these ones' mouths shall flow healing power for the afflicted, shall flow healing power for the mind and heart. Out of these ones' hands shall flow healing power for the sick for I shall birth a heart of compassion such as I walked with on Earth. And even greater shall these do. And these ones, they shall feed the poor of the world. They shall visit the sick. They shall be found ministering in the prisons and their delight is to do the will of My Father.

But not many shall be from the strong and the influential. Oh no indeed, for My glory shall shine through these bruised ones, through these overlooked. And they shall yet bring in a move into My body that shall reflect the hands and the heart of My Father Himself. So repent and humble yourself under the mighty hand of the Lord your God and look well to your ways.

For the **evil one** has sought to hold the whole world in his grasp as the measure of a women is in her appearance and the measure of a man is in his status.

For I grieve for I have seen My Word become an idol in men's hearts.

For I have watched as they have embraced the Book of the Lord and have neglected the Lord of the Book. I have grieved as I have watched My children place My Word even above My person and yet proclaim that they know Me.

Oh no, says the Spirit of the Living God! For knowing the Book of the Lord alone in this next time will not feed you, neither will it give you sustenance. For it is the season to know the Lord of the Book. It is the season to know the Living Word and many, many of My children, too many of My children, have placed in this past season the Book above My person.

But it is only in My presence, it is only as you see Me face to face, it is only by drawing into intimate fellowship and communion with Me that you shall each day receive the manna of life that will lead and guide you through the time to come.

And yes, I hear My children say, 'But Lord we know you through the Word.' And I tell you as I weep for you: No, you know Me not, My children. You know My words and the words of Scripture. But you do not know Me in intimacy. For My voice is still and small, and only those who are tender and intimate, and only those who draw much aside, truly hear Me in this time.

And so I speak to you, beloved. I would lure My Church tenderly apart into their closets, into their chambers, where there are no congregations, where the crowds are gone. That they could once again come and sit before My face and bow before My presence. To call upon Me as beloved, to call upon Me in spirit and in truth as My Church enters into these times. Then My Spirit will start to fall upon My body and the mighty will come forth, for these mighty will be those who are well versed with Me, they will be those who lean on Me for their very breath and sustenance. They are those who know that without My person and without My presence they are nought, for they are only found in Me.

For I tell you that in this day it is no longer Christ in Me, but hear the Spirit of the Living God, it is I am hidden in Christ. And so I will place My hand under their head and I Myself will be their strong right arm for these are the ones who love Me, the ones who love My presence, the ones who love My person.

it is no longer Christ in Me . . .
I am hidden in
Christ

For I am in this endtime calling My body to My person. And it is out of this intimacy with Me, it is out of the love and the consuming passion for My person that My Bride will spring forth.

AND I SAW HEAVEN OPENED, AND BEHOLD A WHITE HORSE; AND HE THAT SAT UPON HIM WAS CALLED FAITHFUL AND TRUE, AND IN RIGHTEOUSNESS HE DOTH JUDGE AND MAKE WAR.

HIS EYES WERE AS A FLAME OF FIRE, AND ON HIS HEAD WERE MANY CROWNS; AND HE HAD A NAME WRITTEN, THAT NO MAN KNEW, BUT HE HIMSELF.

AND HE WAS CLOTHED WITH A VESTURE DIPPED IN BLOOD: AND HIS NAME IS CALLED THE WORD OF GOD.

REVELATION 19:11-13 KJV

For surely it is only when My Bride is hid in Me that she shall be without spot, wrinkle or blemish and so shall the Gospel be preached to all the world and so shall the end come. For My Father comes, the King in all His glory.

Come, come My Bride, draw into your closet. Draw unto Me. For you see, there are many different emphases and many seasons in the body of Christ and so, you teachers take heed that you do not feed My people yesterday's manna.

For the season for self-improvement through the pages of My Word is over, the season of self-absorption and the emphasis on self growing stronger, is finished. For those things that made you strong in this past season will leave you weak and frustrated in this present age. For My Church are on the edge of the end of all things and it is not enough in this time to know only the Book of the Lord. It is only in the embracing of My person that in the next season they will be sustained. Take heed beloved that you do not find that you hunger and thirst. For it is only in knowing My presence, My person and My Word in these coming days that you will be filled.

Oh I grieve as I look to My Church in this day,

For as My eyes pass to and fro across the Earth I see My Church caught up not in things that count for eternity but so ensnared and entangled in the temporal things of this world's system. For indeed the evil one has infiltrated My Church in this past hour, and My sons and My daughters have become ensnared with the pride of life, and indeed it is the pride of life that keeps My ministers from entering into everything destined and ordained for them.

For My children's treasures are treasures of brick and of mortar and of their possessions, and I see the hearts of My ministers ensnared with their building programmes and the activities of ministry and My heart grieves, for their heart is based upon the things that fade away, with the things that do not come from the Father but come from the world itself. For where their treasure is so indeed will their heart be. Yes, and I hear you say, minister, 'No, My heart is not so.'

And I would say to you: My building is not made of bricks and mortar, son, but you have taken much stock of your building when My people have been passed over. But I tell you that the cry of even the smallest of these has not passed unnoticed by My Father.

Oh, for you have business programmes and you teach your men to invest and to plan, and that is good, and it is beneficial. But as I pass by the congregations, I see each man use his faith for his own, for his house and his car, for his stocks and his shares, for the finest. And surely I say unto you minister: Take heed and teach your people, for My prosperity is a prosperity to bless the poor and the lame, to feed the Third World nations, to send My missionaries, to help those less fortunate. But you see the pride of life teaches My people to despise the lesser, and they pat themselves on the head and they mix only in the circles of prosperity and in their heart they despise these lesser ones.

But I tell you, these same ones who have placed their treasure in the things that fade, shall perish with those not of My House as My judgement comes to the world's system. For they shall reap the just reward of the pride of life. And so it shall be that the same stocks and shares which caused them such rejoicing and caused such an elitist spirit, shall cause them to weep. And they shall weep and wail on the day of judgement on the monetary systems of this world.

And they sit in your congregations, Oh minister of the Gospel, they are your elders. Oh minister of the Gospel, they sit on your boards. Oh minister of the Gospel, they are your lunch and dinner companions, Oh minister of the Gospel.

And I tell you, warn them that they may yet repent. Warn them to humble themselves under My mighty hand, that I may yet have mercy upon them. For I came not for the righteous or for the self-sufficient ones. The very ones that these despise in their heart are the very little ones that My Father sent Me to pour out My lifeblood for, these are the ones they so despise.

But for those who have been faithful to My Father in the monetary matters of the Earth, to those who have not set their heart upon the possessions and the riches that I have blessed them with, but have laid up their treasures in Heaven and have given of My substance to feed the poor and those of lesser fortune than themselves—for those who have poured out My substance through the vehicles that I have raised up to preach the Gospel in these endtimes and have given of their substance generously and joyfully with a thankful heart—to these ones comes a multiplication, a multiplication not as in the past. For in the past it was a multiplication of fives and of tens, but in this coming time, says the Lord, I shall multiply My substance supernaturally upon these ones that it shall be a hundred and a thousandfold.

> *Charge them that are rich in this world, that they be not highminded, nor trust in uncertain riches, but in the living God, who giveth us richly all things to enjoy; That they do good, that they be rich in good works, ready to distribute, willing to communicate; Laying up in store for themselves a good foundation against the time to come, that they may lay hold on eternal life.*
> *1 Timothy 6:17-19 (KJV)*

And I shall yet open up unseen riches that until now have been hidden in the secret places of the Earth. And to these ones I shall pour out upon them the gold of Ophir and the treasures of Solomon. I shall pour upon them the gold hidden deep under the Earth and the oil, even the oil shall come into their hands. These will not have to tremble when My judgement falls for I shall keep their substance safe in the eye of the storm. For their substance is indeed My substance and their inheritance is My inheritance. For they are the proven ones, the ones whose treasure is fixed in Me.

And so in these latter days you shall see them come forth as guiding lights rising not from within the world system but rising from out of the world's system. Yes they shall rise. Watch now and see if they will not come forth. And through them My ministers shall be blessed, and shall do their exploits, and through their faithfulness in the hidden places so My Gospel shall yet be financed and shall be preached through all the nations of the Earth. So be it. Amen.

For a great travail rises up from the throne room. A great and terrible cry rises from the Father.

For indeed as My Church stands teetering on the brink of the end of all things, so too, the spirit of treachery has been loosed upon the Earth with vengeance—the spirit of treachery which was spawned by Lucifer in the first Heaven when he with great and violent assault rose up against My Father.

And I tell you, beloved, that it is in this age and in this hour you shall see the spirit of treachery wreak violence upon mankind. And I grieve as I watch and My Father grieves with a great grieving as He watches My body. For as I watch I see the spirit of treachery unleashed with great violence among those of My body. For it is in this season of ministry that the spirit of treachery shall manifest among My Kingdom and through those in ministry as never before.

For truly I tell you that brother in Christ shall rise against brother in Christ, that minister shall rise against minister. That even in this time, the slanders and whispers of deceit rise from My ministers as a tainted incense before My throne as each succumbs to the temptation of the spirit of treachery. And the temptation whispers—as Peter did when he was so tempted: I do not know Him.

And the spirit of treachery whispers as it did to Judas: Sell your

SAUL ATTEMPTS THE LIFE OF DAVID
1 SAMUEL 18:11

brother out for that which is expedient and needful to your ministry. Betray this your brother. Betray this your sister . . . For the spirit of treachery is that most violent of all to manifest against My Church, for was it not the same spirit that drove Lucifer to violent betrayal against Jehovah Himself? And so it has been through the ages—the same spirit of treachery has manifested itself through the one who dipped the bread whilst he supped at My table.

And so it is with you, My son, My daughter. For in your ministry, I see you hold fast to that which is expedient and advantageous to you. And I see you discard day after day that which holds little or no opportunity to further your kingdom. But take heed, Oh minister of the Gospel, take heed and give ear, for what you proclaim to be your kingdom is not My Kingdom. For surely I came not for those who were advantaged, I came not for those who could give you opportunity and status and who could further your ambitions for My Kingdom.

AND THEN SHALL MANY BE OFFENDED, AND SHALL BETRAY ONE ANOTHER, AND SHALL HATE ONE ANOTHER. AND MANY FALSE PROPHETS SHALL RISE, AND SHALL DECEIVE MANY.
AND BECAUSE INIQUITY SHALL ABOUND, THE LOVE OF MANY SHALL WAX COLD. BUT HE THAT SHALL ENDURE UNTO THE END, THE SAME SHALL BE SAVED.
MATTHEW 24:10-13 KJV

Is it not true that I came for the meek and the lowly and for those who had no voice to cry out in the streets? I came for the humble and the poor in spirit. Not many were of wealth or of noble birth or had status.

For again there rises from the throne room a great and terrible grieving from the Father as He weeps for His people. For the spirit of treachery is the spirit of the great betrayer Lucifer. And even as the Father watched as the thirty pieces of silver were traded in that day and wept for My betrayer, so today beloved I weep again for you and I would plead for you who shed innocent blood.

. . . but your invitations are not My invitations and your courts are

not My courts.

How often I have seen you shed innocent blood. For by your well-chosen yet evil words—those words that are only spoken behind closed doors and in private—but as you speak these harsh words, words that are stout against your brother, words that will judge and expose, words that hold no mercy to account, so I tell you, that you have shed innocent blood and I will require of you at My judgement seat an explanation.

For each one seeks his own advantage at the expense of his brother, his sister. For each one seeks his own with such violence that the other is expendable. For honour is not counted among My body and integrity and truth is lacking one to another. And so it is that as long as one is useful to another and your relationships are mutually advantageous, so you dine and invite one another to your courts, but your invitations are not My invitations and your courts are not My courts.

For did I not say go out into the highways and byways? And did I not say judge not a man by what he says or eats or wears or owns? And yet you do all this and hold it much in esteem. And I tell you that your weights are erroneous. And I tell you that you serve not the true Gospel. And I tell you that there shall be an account. There is no sin and nothing so terrible to My Father as this same spirit.

Volume Five

◆ BABYLON ◆

BABYLON FALLEN
REVELATION 18:5

Volume Five

Judgement upon a Renegade Generation

To the disobedient sons of men in this
renegade generation.

To all who hold office whose hearts are engraved with
rebellion, lawlessness and blasphemy against the Most High
God. To those in government, in the mass media, in the
trading systems who exchange truth for delusion and in turn
have mass manufactured the wares of deception from the
secret high places of the Earth to the masses of
twenty-first-century humanity.

For as the peoples of the Earth enter the new
millennium, I tell you, beloved, that as the end of the
age draws near so it is that darkness, great darkness
shall overshadow the Earth and her people.

That a Galiilean carpenter should so claim to be the light of the world, and be so recognised after so many centuries, is best explained on the ground of His divinity.

BERNARD RAMM

Foreword

For the fetters of wickedness shall be unleashed as none of the peoples of the Earth and her nations have ever up until this age experienced, and there shall be a quickening and an increase of the evil one's power and influence upon the nations. For even as it was in the season of the tower of Babel, surely I tell you that the end of all things is at hand and the time of a great outpouring of evil shall pour forth upon the nations. Even those nations that have been at rest and at peace with their neighbours shall indeed start to fear for their livelihood and for the lives of their peoples.

———————◆———————

For I tell you that even as the inhabitants of the Earth have seen violence and wars and rumours of wars in this past time, My Spirit, the Spirit of the Father has held back and arrested the forces of great darkness. But surely My people have forgotten Me, cries the Spirit of the Living God. Surely My people have forsaken their Creator. For have they not made themselves fortresses, fortresses of gold and of silver, fortresses of wood and clay?

———————◆———————

For I weep as I see those I created, the peoples of the nations, turn away from the true and living God and instead worship that which was made by human hands. For My Spirit hovers over the great cities of the Earth—New York, London, Tokyo—the great machinations and plans of man and mammon, the buying, the selling and the trading. And so, it is in this season, at the birth of the twenty-first century, that as My hand stretches across the nations and population groups of the Earth, that JUDGEMENT SHALL DESCEND ON THE PROPAGATORS OF INIQUITY.

———◆———

But as I judge I weep. Yes as My Father judges, He weeps. For it does not have to be this way. And I rend My Heart before you, My sons, My daughters, for even though you have not acknowledged Me, nothing, no nothing can separate My love from you and so I send you My apostles, I send you My prophets, I send you My mighty messengers—those who proclaim My Name in the highways and the byways—yet still you turn your ear from Me and your hearts stay far from Me. Repent, before it is too late, repent.

Then I saw another angel descending from Heaven, possessing great authority, and the earth was illuminated with His radiance and splendour.

And he shouted with a mighty voice, She is fallen! Mighty Babylon is fallen! She has become a resort and dwelling place for demons, a dungeon haunted by every loathsome spirit, an abode for every filthy and detestable bird.

For all nations have drunk the wine of her passionate unchastity, and the rulers and leaders of the earth have joined with her in committing fornication (idolatry), and the businessmen of the earth have become rich with the wealth of her excessive luxury and wantonness.

I then heard another voice from heaven saying, Come out from her, my people, so that you may not share in her sins, neither participate in her plagues.

For her iniquities (her crimes and transgressions) are piled up as high as heaven, and God has remembered her wickedness and (her) crimes (and calls them up for settlement).

Repay to her what she herself has paid (to others) and double (her doom) in accordance with what she has done. Mix a double portion for her in the cup she mixed (for others).

So shall her plagues (afflictions, calamities) come thick upon her in a single day, pestilence and anguish and sorrow and famine; and she shall be utterly consumed (burned up with fire) for mighty is the Lord God Who judges her.

Revelation 18:1-6,8

The Amplified Bible

◆ JUDGEMENT UPON THE MEDIA ◆

PROPHETIC WORD RECEIVED NOVEMBER 1999

And so too My wrath is turned upon the pedlars and the soothsayers of this day. And it is you, the media, I hold accountable.

For even in these past thirty years, surely you have propagated lies and bombarded My people day and night with your lies until the truth they once knew and embraced in their hearts was in turn exchanged for a lie.

But the lie was your lie, manufactured and propagated by those great empires built by mankind. And so it was, that that which was originally birthed to glorify what was good and righteous and pure in the human heart became overtaken by the lust for money, power and greed. And avarice reared its head. And so the media empires of this world became tools to manipulate and control and exercise dominion over the public at large, over this generation.

And it is you, newspaper magnates and you, television network magnates, it is you, Hollywood, it is you, computer magnates that I, the Living God, hold accountable. For surely you have taken that which was invented with the express aim to communicate that which was wholesome and to build the fabric of society, but you have, in this last

BUT WHOSO SHALL OFFEND ONE OF THESE LITTLE ONES WHICH BELIEVE IN ME, IT WERE BETTER FOR HIM THAT A MILLSTONE WERE HANGED ABOUT HIS NECK, AND THAT HE WERE DROWNED IN THE DEPTH OF THE SEA.
MATTHEW 18:6 KJV

generation, been the propagators of death and of violence, of destruction, of moral decay and of every evil known to mankind. And so you have in turn torn asunder the very fabric of mankind and in its place you have left emptiness and lust and avarice and divorce and fornication and murder.

I tell you that there comes a time drawing nigh upon the Earth when even your very soul shall be required of you. You have been found wanting. Yes, says the one sovereign God, you have been found wanting. And as you stand before My Throne, yet shall there come a time when you shall give account of your empire. You shall stand before those that raped and those that were the fornicators and you shall give account for the pornographic material you broadcast. For each rape and each abuse shall be held to your account, Oh man.

And you shall stand before those that were murdered, those whose blood cries out for justice and you shall give account, Oh man, you shall give account before the heavenly host and the Son of Man. For you broadcast lust and you broadcast violence, which in turn fed lust and fed the violent until they no longer could contain themselves within the bounds of human decency and what they knew to be right and proper.

And so they raped, Oh man. And they murdered, Oh man. But was it not I who said whoever causes one of these to stumble . . . Yes you have caused My little ones to stumble by feeding them day by day REBELLION from your screens. You fed them REBELLION,

LAWLESSNESS and BLASPHEMY, until lawlessness was written in their hearts. It would have been better that a millstone was put around your neck, Oh son of disobedience.

And then you took the faithful and across your screens you mocked their faith. You exchanged faith for humanism and intellectualism and atheism and many, many of My little ones fell and followed your lies. And so I tell you, Oh man, that your judgement awaits. The Son of Man is seated on the great white throne and His angels stand like flaming fire.

FOR YOU BROADCAST LUST AND YOU BROADCAST VIOLENCE, WHICH IN TURN FED LUST AND FED THE VIOLENT UNTIL THEY NO LONGER COULD CONTAIN THEMSELVES WITHIN THE BOUNDS OF HUMAN DECENCY AND WHAT THEY KNEW TO BE RIGHT AND PROPER.

So repent, Oh man, while there is yet time. Repent, Oh man, before you take your last breath and are damned for eternity. Repent, Oh man, that I do not hold you accountable for the millions of souls that have perished because of your disobedience.

For much, yes, so very much was given you and from you, much was required. And as I watch you, in your self-deception and your delusions, I weep for you. For My warning to you is My mercy. Repent Oh man, repent Oh child, repent. You who I created to serve and to love Me, repent. Repent even today in your rejection of Me. I wait for you. I weep. I weep and wait for you each and every day. Repent, BELOVED man.

◆ JUDGEMENT UPON THE POLITICIANS ◆

PROPHETIC WORD RECEIVED NOVEMBER 1999

And so it is you—the presidents, governors, the leaders of the Earth—it is you kings and queens and princes, it is you who must be brought to account.

For to those who have ruled with the rod of wisdom and the rod of justice, for to those who have ruled with the rod of truth and the rod of grace, for to you kings, queens and presidents who have dealt a just measure and have ruled with prudence—to you who have served the Kingdom that was entrusted to you and have not served mammon or men's favour or selfish ambition—to you shall be entrusted the powers of the age to come.

To you whose voice I have heard raised to Me in the night hours crying out for wisdom for those you govern—to you I shall be known as wisdom and to you I shall be your strong right arm of governance. For you have sought My ways and you have established My precepts, and you have passed My laws and you have stood against that which opposes My ways, and you have raised your voice against that which is unjust and you have established justice even in the streets of your nations—justice has been established.

But to you who have been unfaithful stewards of the nations of the Earth—you have done that which ought not to have been done and you have left undone those things which ought to have been done. For like Pilate, you have washed your hands clean of the blood of those foetuses murdered in the name of democracy. For like those who have gone before you, you have shrugged your shoulders and have said, 'It is modern times.'

But I tell you, Oh leader, that on the night that your life expires, you too shall stand before My throne to give account for the laws passed under your time in office. And I tell you this day that no amount of cleansing shall clean your soul of the blood of the innocents. For you did not stand up for what you knew in your conscience to be right. For your voice was not heard in protest in the streets.

But the blood of the unborn cried out to the heavens and their cries were not disregarded by Me. And I rent My garments as abortion clinic after abortion clinic opened their doors. And thousands by thousands, the sacred breath of life given to all men was extinguished across the nations. And it is you, yes you, Western powers, that I hold most accountable. For surely I tell you, you have taken the Third World countries and you have exemplified unrighteousness. And so you exchanged guns and lawlessness in your schools in place of morning prayer, and you replaced faith in Me with faith in

> THEN I SAW A GREAT WHITE THRONE AND THE ONE WHO WAS SEATED UPON IT,
> FROM WHOSE PRESENCE AND FROM THE SIGHT OF WHOSE FACE EARTH AND SKY FLED AWAY, AND NO PLACE WAS FOUND FOR THEM.
> I (ALSO) SAW THE DEAD, GREAT AND SMALL; THEY STOOD BEFORE THE THRONE, AND BOOKS WERE OPENED. THEN ANOTHER BOOK WAS OPENED, WHICH IS (THE BOOK) OF LIFE. AND THE DEAD WERE JUDGED (SENTENCED) BY WHAT THEY HAD DONE (THEIR WHOLE WAY OF FEELING AND ACTING, THEIR AIMS AND ENDEAVOURS) IN ACCORDANCE WITH WHAT WAS RECORDED IN THE BOOKS.
> REVELATION 20: 11-12
> THE AMPLIFIED BIBLE

those who never claimed deity, and so a generation was birthed—a generation who neither acknowledged nor worshipped Me—and then you watched in horror as the massacres occurred. But you did not change your ways.

And so you swore allegiance behind closed doors to those nations to whom it was expedient—but you did not consult Me, Oh man, and so I saw you as you made your pacts with the representatives of hell itself. And you said that it was right and you said that it was good. But it was not right, Oh man. And it was not good, Oh man. And I saw as you sold nations, even continents out in the presidential suites and in the corridors of power for that which was convenient and expedient and was politically correct, that would bring you favour and votes in your next term. But what was expedient and what was political shall be a wrench around your neck in the coming days. For I tell you that in these latter times so shall your office even be wrested out of your hands. And even that power which you guard so jealously shall be taken from you. Even in a moment of time. So it shall be.

THE CONFUSION OF TONGUES
GENESIS 11:4,8

◆ JUDGEMENT UPON THE WORLD'S TRADING SYSTEMS ◆

PROPHETIC WORD RECEIVED NOVEMBER 1999

For I tell you, indeed I declare to you the things that have yet to take place upon the Earth, before the time of the great tribulation.

For the Depression of 1929 shall be as nothing in comparison to the losses and devastation that shall strike the stock markets of the world stage in the years ahead. For I tell you that as each man to himself has trusted in and placed his trust in idols of gold and of silver, so shall the judgements start to rain down.

So it shall be as in the twinkling of an eye that the stock markets and the trading systems of the great nations shall, even in a matter of a forty-eight-hour period, collapse. That every man who for himself has laid up great treasure, shall in this season be reduced to nothing.

For that which man has placed his trust in, will fail him. The trading systems of this world, which men have been told are infallible, shall prove themselves tenuous at the least and shall be the ruin of many millions in the years to come. And the ruin shall come greater upon those who have placed much faith in the arm of man. For I prophesy that the stock markets of the Western and Eastern world shall fall. And as they fall, so devastation shall strike the world's economy. And so those who have trusted in the wealth of man to save them, shall finally see their idols for what they are. They shall say: We are brought down to nothing, as in a day; that which we were told could not be, has happened in a day.

And so a great terror shall strike at the heart of those who have ruled the nations by control and manipulation—by trade and by extortion—as they see their idols collapse before them. And so the great shaking and judgements upon the Earth shall begin.

For I have warned My people, says the Lord. I warned them in the days of Noah, I warned them in the days of Sodom. I warned them at Babel but still, says the Lord, the Sovereign and One True God, still My people rebelled against Me. And their hearts strayed from Me and their thoughts wandered far from Me. And as I searched the cities of My great and beloved Earth, surely it was only a remnant that I saw. A remnant that looked out for My interests and yearned for My appearing.

And so in these end days, My heart burns within Me and becomes vexed. For through the centuries they killed My prophets. And even now My prophets are despised. And so this last generation they have made themselves idols out of their hands, and they have turned away from Me. They worship idols of wood and clay—their homes, automobiles—and they worship idols of gold and silver. They exchange the worship of Me, the Living God, for that of stocks and shares and gold and bonds—for the worship of oil and armaments.

They have exchanged their souls for that which cannot save them. For so it is that as their life expires, all they have amassed in the high places of the Earth, all their idols shall stand silent.

Their merchandise is of gold, silver, precious stones, and pearls; of fine linen, purple, silk, and scarlet (stuffs); all kinds of scented wood, all sorts of articles of ivory, all varieties of objects of costly woods, bronze, iron and marble;

Of cinnamon, spices, incense, ointment and perfume, and frankincense, of wine and olive oil, fine flour and wheat; of cattle and sheep, horses and conveyances; and of slaves (the bodies) and souls of men!

The ripe fruits and delicacies for which your soul longed have gone from you, and all your luxuries and dainties, your elegance and splendour are lost to you, never again to be recovered or experienced!

The dealers who handled these articles, who grew wealthy through their business with her, will stand a long way off, in terror of her doom and torment, weeping and grieving aloud, and saying,

Alas, alas for the great city was robed in fine linen, in purple and scarlet, bedecked and glittering with gold, with precious stones, and with pearls!

Because in one (single) hour all the vast wealth has been destroyed (wiped out). And all ship captains and pilots, navigators and all who live by seafaring, the crews and all who ply their trade on the sea, stood a long way off.

Revelation 18:12-17

The Amplified Bible

PROPHETIC WORD RECEIVED NOVEMBER 1999

Oh and as I watch you, man of the cloth, I see the great institutions that you have birthed in the name of My Father and in the name of the Son and My heart is torn.

For the whitewashed politicians that stand and speak in My Name—yes My Name is on their lips but their hearts and minds are far from Me—and so they have used My Name and have thus accrued power and sway among the leaders and the politicians and those bankers that rule with sway and with power on the Earth.

But I tell you in truth it is as it was when I walked the Earth. For the knowledge of Me and the knowledge of My Kingdom is far from them. Hypocrites, I know your hearts for I see and discern the motives and intents of your hearts. And so it is that at this turn of the twenty-first century, so it is that religion has become one of the influential traders of the Earth. And the great wealth that has been amassed to the institutional Church through the centuries surely has made you a formidable and a ruthless opponent. But Oh, man of the cloth, you who lead your followers to the damned—

LET US HEAR THE CONCLUSION OF THE WHOLE MATTER: FEAR GOD, AND KEEP HIS COMMANDMENTS: FOR THIS IS THE WHOLE DUTY OF MAN. FOR GOD SHALL BRING EVERY WORK INTO JUDGMENT, WITH EVERY SECRET THING, WHETHER IT BE GOOD, OR WHETHER IT BE EVIL.
ECCLESIASTES 12:13-14 KJV

you the propagators of bribery, the corrupt practices that you engage in behind your closed but very powerful doors, the deals made among the heads of state and among those even more powerful but far more hidden, those deals that turn the politics of nations—it is to you that I speak.

FOR YOU HAVE JOINED YOURSELF AS A WHORE TO THOSE WHOSE OCCUPATION IS THE SHEDDING OF BLOOD AND YOU HAVE TRADED WITH THE SUBSTANCES OF THE EAST AND THE ARMS OF THE WEST.

And I tell you that worse it will be for you than for those who dwelt in the cities of Sodom and Gomorrah. For surely their sin was open and bared before all, but you, Oh harlot, how much innocent blood has dripped from your hands in the name of My Church, in the name of the Son—your sin, your lies, your extortions, your harlotry has been hidden in the secret places of the Earth. Your lewd practices have been seen by no man and no man ever lived to tell the tales of exposure. For you have joined yourself as a whore to those whose occupation is the shedding of blood and you have traded with the substances of the East and the arms of the West. You have traded in violence, you have traded in murder, you have traded in extortion, you have traded with the lives of the innocent and of the oppressed . . .

You have liberated those who have oppressed the innocent and unprotected. And surely this day I adjure you. I am against you, Oh man of the cloth. I am against you and your detestable practices. Better it was that you had no knowledge of aught to do with My

Name than what you have done And so it shall be that I have spewed you out of My mouth. For in you there is no repentance. In you there is no sorrow and there stands for you no restitution.

Oh, man of the cloth, you whose robes are stained with the blood of the innocents. I require judgement. And judgement shall take its turn.

Oh, man of the cloth, you whose robes are stained with the blood of the innocents. I require judgement. And judgement shall take its turn.

◆ TO THE POLITICIANS, LAWYERS, MEDIA MOGULS, BUSINESS EXECUTIVES AND ALL WHO HAVE FORGOTTEN ◆

PROPHETIC WORD RECEIVED NOVEMBER 1999

For I walk through the cities of this Earth where you do your deal making, My son.

And it is as I pass you by, beloved, that My cheeks are hot with tears shed for you. For indeed has it not been I who was beside you even from when you were a child? Has it not been My presence that was with you when in the travail of your soul you cried out? And in the valley of the shadow when none knew your agony of heart, was I not beside you, child? Was it not strange that those coincidences that delivered you from events that could have destroyed the course of your life were in parallel to those nights when you cried out to Me?

But as you grew in years, in the knowledge of worldly things, My son, your heart once tender and open to Me became hardened and your conscience seared. And so as you grew in the ways of a perverse and thankless generation, you rejected faith as you knew it. And you threw Me aside as a childish thing.

Yet still in your times of greatest pain you would call out to Me. And in great compassion I would come to you and you would know My comfort. But then the

> THEY WILL STAND A LONG WAY OFF, IN TERROR OF HER TORMENT, AND THEY WILL CRY, WOE AND ALAS, THE GREAT CITY, THE MIGHTY CITY, BABYLON! IN ONE SINGLE HOUR HOW YOUR DOOM (JUDGEMENT) HAS OVERTAKEN YOU!
> AND EARTH'S BUSINESSMEN WILL WEEP AND GRIEVE OVER HER BECAUSE NO-ONE BUYS THEIR FREIGHT (CARGO) ANYMORE.
> REVELATION 18:10-11
> THE AMPLIFIED BIBLE

morning light would dawn and memories of Me would fade. And so you grew in your own self-sufficiency.

And so it came, My son, that through the passage of time you started to look upon Me and Mine with cynicism. And your heart became jaded and filled with unbelief. And so it was that you rationalised that you had indeed put away childish things, and so embraced the atheisms of a perverse generation and you rejected Me.

But still I was there as an onlooker, weeping for you, calling you tenderly until you closed the door to your heart completely. I watched over the years as you strove to find your way alone through the ruthlessness of life around you.

You tentatively reached out to love, then learned that risk hurt you. And so the first of your barriers was erected and then the second and third, until love was a disregarded ideal, until you became as much the abuser as the abused.

And still I watched you, as you rose up the ranks of society and learned the fine art of disguise. And how well you wore your masks. And I watched as you mastered the lies until truth became so distorted that even the lies seemed like truth and the truth was despised.

And so now, My child, held in such high esteem by a renegade generation—you hold your position—you have achieved many desires and many goals have been accomplished. And so you say in your heart: I have lost faith. And you scoff behind their backs at those few who still hold on to the vestiges of faith amidst the masses filled with cynicism and unbelief.

Yet, still some nights, I enter your household and silently, unnoticed by you, I stand by your bedside. And I watch the hardness on your face ease as weariness enfolds you and the stresses and strains of all that encompasses your life today dissolve away in sleep's deep respite. And I too remember a time when in your tender years you held out your heart to Me in wonder and in innocence. And it is as I remember—Oh great politician, lawyer, media mogul, executive—so esteemed by the society who does your bidding . . .

It is as I remember that the tears course down My face for you.

For you see, My son . . .you did not lose faith . . .

you lost Me.

Volume Six

◆ THE FATHER ◆

THE NEW JERUSALEM
REVELATION 21:2

Volume Six

The Son's Endtime Revelation
of the Father to the Church

And now dearest child, it is to you that I would speak. For surely over all the years past, has it not been I who gently took you by your hand and whose guiding presence you sensed through so many desert places?

And yes, My dearest child, surely even in those times of serving Me—when much seemed barren and when the raging tempest threatened to overwhelm you—surely it was I and My holy angels who raised Our standard on your behalf and calmed the storm?

◆

It has been that in your walk with Me upon the Earth in this past Church age, that you grew to know My Ways and you grew to know My Book and you grew to know My Voice in more intimacy and greater sensitivity.

But now as I stand with My hands outstretched to you, I have come to take you on the Last Great Journey. And even now as you sense My Person and My Presence so unmistakably and you reach out your hand and place it in Mine— know this—that I Myself have come to lead you out of this present Church age and beyond the veil that you may know the Power and the Glory and the Majesty and the Terror and the all-consuming passion that My Father holds for you. For surely, the last and most glorious of revelations has been held back for this very day and for this endtime hour of the Church—the Revelation of My Father.

> THE PERSON WHO HAS MY COMMANDS AND KEEPS THEM IS THE ONE WHO REALLY LOVES ME; AND WHOEVER REALLY LOVES ME WILL BE LOVED BY MY FATHER AND I TOO WILL LOVE HIM AND WILL SHOW, MANIFEST MYSELF TO HIM. (I WILL LET MYSELF BE CLEARLY SEEN BY HIM AND MAKE MYSELF REAL TO HIM.)
> JOHN 14:21
> THE AMPLIFIED BIBLE.

And so, this day I walk among the cities of the Earth seeking, seeking for those who love to be with Us. Seeking for those whose hearts hunger for Our Presence. It is to these that the powers of the ages to come shall be entrusted—to these, the friends of the Father and the friends of the Son and His Spirit.

And so this day I walk among the cities of the Earth seeking, seeking for those

who love to be with Us. Seeking for those whose hearts hunger for Our presence

It is to these that the powers of the ages to come shall be entrusted

Oh, beloved child, surely if you have seen Me truly, you will have seen My Father.

For there is none like unto Him. All I am is found in Him and He is found in Me. And beloved, in this coming season, it is not enough to know My name. It is not enough to know My Word.

But as you draw near to Me and come and enter into My presence, you shall receive a revelation of My Father. For you cannot see Me in truth, you cannot worship Me in spirit and in truth and not see and recognise and know the Father. For I and the Father are One.

And so it has been in these past seasons of My body, that My Church and My ministers have come only to the outskirts of My person. They have entered only into the outer courts of My glory and few there are that walk the Earth. And few there are that are My ministers today, few there are that have passed beyond that veil. But the winds of My Spirit have blown and now that shall change. For I am raising up those that are called by My Name— they are the ones that shall press through to the Father. These are the ones that continue to worship Me through all the pressures and the strains and pay the price of life in this realm that grows darker month by month. These are the ones that so hunger for My person. These are the ones that so thirst for My presence. These are the ones who rest their head upon My bosom. And so these are the ones that I embrace with My right hand.

And it is to these in this season that a great revelation shall descend upon them. And I tell you that to these ones who have been found faithful, to these ones who have been tested and have been tried in the furnace of affliction and have clung to Me in the secret place, so shall there descend from the very throne of Heaven itself, a mighty stirring.

For I tell you, that in this day, so the Father stirs Himself to come and fellowship, to come and make His abode with His people—to come and reveal Himself to those who love His Son, to those who love My person. For it is coming, the season of the Father and the Father, the Glorious one, the Creator of Heaven and Earth and all that exists beyond Heaven and under the Earth.

So it is that in this time, the Father Himself shall arise. And in your closets and in your secret chambers, those who have truly loved Me, those who love My presence more than they have loved their own ambitions, those who have loved My presence more than they have loved their ministry, to those who have loved to be with Me, more than they love to be used by Me. It is to these that the Father shall reveal His

NEITHER PRAY I FOR THESE ALONE, BUT FOR THEM ALSO WHICH SHALL BELIEVE ON ME THROUGH THEIR WORD; THAT THEY ALL MAY BE ONE; AS THOU, FATHER, ART IN ME, AND I IN THEE, THAT THEY ALSO MAY BE ONE IN US: THAT THE WORLD MAY BELIEVE THAT THOU HAST SENT ME.

AND THE GLORY WHICH THOU GAVEST ME I HAVE GIVEN THEM; THAT THEY MAY BE ONE, EVEN AS WE ARE ONE: I IN THEM, AND THOU IN ME, THAT THEY MAY BE MADE PERFECT IN ONE; AND THAT THE WORLD MAY KNOW THAT THOU HAST SENT ME, AND HAST LOVED THEM, AS THOU HAST LOVED ME.

FATHER, I WILL THAT THEY ALSO, WHOM THOU HAST GIVEN ME, BE WITH ME WHERE I AM; THAT THEY MAY BEHOLD MY GLORY, WHICH THOU HAST GIVEN ME: FOR THOU LOVEDST ME BEFORE THE FOUNDATION OF THE WORLD.

JOHN 17:20-24 KJV

majesty and His consuming passion for His Creation.

And so, My beloved ones, as you draw unto Me in worship and in adoration, I tell you that in this time, so the Father shows Himself. So the Father Himself stirs from His throne towards these ones that I love. And the glory and the radiance and the majesty of His person shall descend upon these ones.

The glory and the power, and the power, and the power, and the power, and the majesty, shall start to fall as a mantle. And the fear of Him shall descend. And the awe of His person shall fall. And I tell you, His love, His love, His everlasting mercies, His great compassions, shall overshadow His beloved as a mantle, thick with

. . . THOSE WHO LOVE MY PRESENCE
MORE THAN THEY HAVE
LOVED THEIR OWN AMBITIONS,
THOSE WHO HAVE LOVED MY PRESENCE
MORE THAN THEY HAVE LOVED THEIR MINISTRY,
TO THOSE WHO HAVE LOVED TO BE WITH ME,
MORE THAN THEY LOVE TO BE USED BY ME.
IT IS TO THESE THAT THE FATHER SHALL REVEAL
HIS MAJESTY AND HIS CONSUMING PASSION FOR
His Creation

His glory. And they shall know the love of My Father.

For even as My Father loves the Son, Oh, how My Father's hands and heart are outstretched to His Creation. Oh, there is none like My Father. Oh, how I would that My Church would know My Father. Oh, how I would that My body would embrace My Father. He is My very breath. There is none like unto Him. And He is coming to His people. He comes swiftly to His people.

For as the Father speaks, it is as though the whole world would stop in His wake.

Oh, to hear the voice of the Father is to hear that which is beyond all wonder, beyond human imagination. For child of God, His very voice and heart echoes love such as you and I, in our frail mortality, cannot begin to comprehend—His care, His concern, His mercy, His compassions—as they fall on us.

For He knows that we are but dust. And even our very frailties and weaknesses, He understands . . .

And so it is the Father who in this season would take your hand and mine. And so it is His whisper would become a crescendo in the hearts and the minds of His servants in this generation. As He thunders out of the glory and the majesty. And out of the winds of His presence, He would gently bid you nearer. And He would whisper:

It is I.

THE FOLLOWING VISION IS
THE RESULT OF A PERSONAL
VISITATION TO
THE AUTHOR.

For it is to you in these times that the Father would be revealed, not only in His great and His fierce and terrible glory and majesty that all humanity would fling themselves prostrate before His Almighty throne in Heaven as dust, for such it is true the whole Earth and His Creation is before Him.

But in His incredible all-consuming and passionate love for us, His sons and His daughters—at the same time He has chosen to reveal His most terrible and awesome majesty and power—so it is, children of the endtime Church, that He would reveal Himself in this last age as Abba, Daddy, Father.

When I was crying out to the Father for the ability to translate all that I have experienced He is into the natural, no words, no attempt seemed able to match all that is to be found and encompasses His incredible presence. In the midst of my seeming inability to convey the completely amazing wonder of being with Him as Father and Daddy, I heard Him laugh that unmistakable tender laugh and sensed His eyes twinkle with that all-knowing, long-suffering humour. (Oh, for how our

Father loves to laugh!) And I heard Him whisper: Beloved child, just tell others how you have experienced Heaven and how you have experienced Me and in turn there shall be a great impartation of My immense and infinite love and yearning for them. And so I will pour out My Spirit upon them that they too might cry out to My throne—Abba, Abba Daddy—and I shall reveal Myself in My great mercies and My tender compassions to them, that My Church might know Me.

There have been several times that I have seen the Father and His wonderful Heaven as an inner vision, but I felt Him ask me to share one occasion when it seemed that at this particular season in my life, the testings, the tribulations and even the temptations were so fierce that I felt far from holy, far from worthy. I had not graced the throne room for some weeks and I was feeling somewhat condemned, not particularly spiritual at all, being totally consumed with the activities of ministry.

But you see, dear saint, that is exactly the object lesson that the Father would have us understand. His love for us is not based on human conditions and parameters for good behaviour. Yes, He must judge the sin. But His love for you and for me is so passionate, so all-consuming that it is almost impossible to comprehend the length and the breadth of it. The incredible thing about the Father's love is that He IS our Father, even the greatest most loving earthly father is merely a shadow of our great Father of fathers. He knows that we are dust, He puts up with our idiosyncracies and our humanities like a father whose patience and infinite understanding knows no end.

He is all beautiful. He is everything that you and I, since we were babes in arms, have ever dreamed of. And He is forever consumed with His everlasting love for you.

Bless the LORD, O my soul. O LORD my God, thou art very great; thou art clothed with honour and majesty.
Who coverest thyself with light as with a garment: who stretchest out the heavens like a curtain:
Who layeth the beams of his chambers in the waters: who maketh the clouds his chariot: who walketh upon the wings of the wind:

Psalm 104:1-3 KJV

The throne room was so huge, so magnificent, that it seemed to stretch for miles into infinity. I was led there by Jesus, my brother, the great lover of my soul. And so we stood on the outskirts, almost at a doorway and entrance to the great throne room. I turned to Jesus, He that is most beautiful, the fairest of ten thousand in whose eyes it seems that all the compassions and understandings of all the eons of Earth belong.

And as I looked into His eyes, I saw His terrible grief for the peoples of the Earth, His incredible tenderness and love for His Church and for those of His Household and yet such a deep desperate grieving for that which is His Bride as He watches her entangled with the spirit of the world strangling her. But as He looked at me, the sadness still in His eyes . . . suddenly, a radiant light and joy came again across His countenance and I know that His thoughts were with His most beloved—His breath—His very heartbeat—His Father.

For there is not a moment when the Son does not think about the Father; there is not a second when the concerns of the Father do not concern the Son. And there is not a moment when the Father's thoughts are not with His beloved, His only begotten—obedient even unto death by crucifixion. And how they love the Spirit, the Holy Spirit, the great transmitter of all that the Father and the Son think and will and do.

And so it is that the brilliance on Jesus' countenance grew brighter and more intense and slowly—Oh so slowly— He turned His face to me and smiled and it seemed that the whole of Heaven's joy was in that smile. And His eyes shone brilliantly with such an exhilaration and excitement and with the anticipation of His Father's presence. And so it is that He threw his head back and laughed with an unspoilt child's delight. And I knew that He had heard from the One He loved more than life itself—His beloved Father and that He had been called to Him.

Then Jesus turned to me and took my hand: The Father Himself loves you. He would speak with you. And Jesus and I exchanged the look that brother and sister would exchange, that only they would understand, the love shared between them for a beloved parent.

Oh, for although I knew in my frail humanity that I could

surely only feel but a shadow of the unimaginable adoration that Jesus the Son holds for the Father, I knew that since that day many years before when I cried out to the Father of Jesus Christ Himself to reveal Himself to me, I had been unendingly desperately in love with Him—my Father—Abba—my Daddy.

As Jesus and I stood at the entrance of that most glorious room from which exuded a brilliance of light, I could hardly make out any defined shapes except a magnified magnificent brilliance that seemed to be miles off, which I knew in my heart to be the Father's throne.

Jesus took my hand in His and together we stepped through the entrance. Immediately my senses were engulfed with the myriad sounds and sensations of Heaven. Jesus and I kept walking. It seemed as though we walked slowly, still miles from the brilliant pulsating light of my Father's throne.

As we walked it seemed as though we passed thousands of people on either side of the huge aisle, maybe even millions and millions of people. I could not make out any defined shapes or figures, I just somehow knew that these were some of the great cloud of witnesses that we were passing by, all our attention completely riveted towards the Father's brilliance.

As we started to draw nearer to the throne, although still a long way off, the roaring from the throne area became louder and more intense, and it became harder to walk, because of the thickness and awesomeness of the glory that radiated from the throne. It felt as though to put one foot in front of the other was like walking through glory, through the manifest presence and cloak of the Father's radiance.

But still we walked. And Jesus kept at my pace. But all His attention was fixed on the One He loves—was riveted towards the blinding form of the Father who has His whole attention. And it seemed that in that moment my heart had joined with the heart of the Son and both our hearts were as one in adoration of the Father. And suddenly Jesus' words in John 14 took on a new meaning and I realised that as the Church, we had almost

FOR HE KNOWETH OUR FRAME; HE REMEMBERETH THAT WE ARE DUST.
PSALM 103:10-14 KJV

forgotten that the only reason that Jesus came to Earth was to reveal His Father. And Jesus turned to me: 'Tell My Church,' He said, His voice almost close to tears with yearning. And it became a command: 'Tell My endtime Church that I came to reveal My Father.'

And suddenly, I was on my own. And as I neared the throne area, an overwhelming cry to my Father burst from my heart—and my longing for Him, the great Father of compassions and the tender Father of mercies was so intense that when my mouth opened, the cry was soundless. And it was at that time it seemed all else disappeared apart from me and my Father. And I knew that as I had been walking, even stumbling my way up the aisle of the great throne room through the thick glory, that even as the Father and that great cloud of witnesses were watching me, they saw a wounded and bloodied

CAN A WOMAN FORGET HER SUCKING CHILD, THAT SHE SHOULD NOT HAVE COMPASSION ON THE SON OF HER WOMB? YEA, THEY MAY FORGET, YET WILL I NOT FORGET THEE.

BEHOLD, I HAVE GRAVEN THEE UPON THE PALMS OF MY HANDS; THY WALLS ARE CONTINUALLY BEFORE ME.

ISAIAH 49:15-16 KJV

soldier, bleeding and bruised from the war in the trenches, covered in the filth of the enemy's lies and of my own disobedience, my uniform tattered and torn and filthy—and again I knew that I had, in my own strength, as a soldier in the beginnings of this great endtimes battle, failed Him so miserably. And in my gross humanity, I half expected my Father to withdraw from me.

But as I drew, oh so slowly nearer, dragging one foot in front of the other, crying because of the glory and the incredible yearning for Him, so I saw the Father stir. And so I saw the Father Himself, the great King of the Universe slowly in all His power and majesty rise from His throne. And where the angels and Heaven had been absorbed in Heaven and the universe's business and in worship of Him, I saw the Father raise His magnificent right hand. And suddenly, the whole of Heaven hushed and a great stillness descended. And it was then that I knew that the whole of Heaven's attention—but far more that my beloved Father's attention—was on one figure and one figure alone—on His wounded, frail, stumbling soldier before Him.

And then I knew my Father—the great King of Heaven—

was weeping for me, not out of pity, but out of His terrible yearning for me—His beloved. And I saw Him slowly raise His right hand. And He held His right hand before His face, I could not see His face but I knew beyond any doubt that He was weeping as He held His hand to His lips and Oh so gently kissed the palm of His hand. Then ever so tenderly, I saw Him reach out His hand palm outward towards me. And I saw my name imprinted on the palm of His hand.

And then He whispered my name. And in that whisper burned His tender terrible all-consuming love for me. And in that whisper was the balm of Gilead and the Rose of Sharon and I could do nothing but bow down prostrate on the ground—for His brilliance and His yearning for me were too terrible.

I felt Him lift me and draw me to Himself and my face was buried in His embrace and it seemed like I was drowning in His all-consuming love for me. And He held me—it felt like for all eternity—and again He whispered my name and I felt His tears fall onto my hands and onto my hair.

And still I clung to Him. And still He held me. And

Heaven waited.

For all eyes were focused on the Father. And the Father's eyes were focused on me, His child, His beloved, His Bride. And it was in that embrace that all sin was washed away, all weariness was erased, all wounds were healed and I knew that I would never rest again until that day when for all time I would be with Him where He is—and that He would have my heart for eternity and I would have His.

I BEHELD TILL THE THRONES WERE CAST DOWN, AND THE ANCIENT OF DAYS DID SIT, WHOSE GARMENT WAS WHITE AS SNOW, AND THE HAIR OF HIS HEAD LIKE THE PURE WOOL: HIS THRONE WAS LIKE THE FIERY FLAME, AND HIS WHEELS AS BURNING FIRE. A FIERY STREAM ISSUED AND CAME FORTH FROM BEFORE HIM: THOUSAND THOUSANDS MINISTERED UNTO HIM, AND TEN THOUSAND TIMES TEN THOUSAND STOOD BEFORE HIM: THE JUDGMENT WAS SET, AND THE BOOKS WERE OPENED. I BEHELD THEN BECAUSE OF THE VOICE OF THE GREAT WORDS WHICH THE HORN SPAKE: I BEHELD EVEN TILL THE BEAST WAS SLAIN, AND HIS BODY DESTROYED, AND GIVEN TO THE BURNING FLAME.

AS CONCERNING THE REST OF THE BEASTS, THEY HAD THEIR DOMINION TAKEN AWAY: YET THEIR LIVES WERE PROLONGED FOR A SEASON AND TIME.

I SAW IN THE NIGHT VISIONS, AND, BEHOLD, ONE LIKE THE SON OF MAN CAME WITH THE CLOUDS OF HEAVEN, AND CAME TO THE ANCIENT OF DAYS, AND THEY BROUGHT HIM NEAR BEFORE HIM.

AND THERE WAS GIVEN HIM DOMINION, AND GLORY, AND A KINGDOM, THAT ALL PEOPLE, NATIONS, AND LANGUAGES, SHOULD SERVE HIM: HIS DOMINION IS AN EVERLASTING DOMINION, WHICH SHALL NOT PASS AWAY, AND HIS KINGDOM THAT WHICH SHALL NOT BE DESTROYED.

DANIEL 7:10-14 KJV

Volume Seven

♦ LAST DAY'S ASSIGNMENTS
AGAINST THE ELECT ♦

Volume Seven

'My children perish.' Jesus' voice was soft—so soft that it was barely audible. And then He turned to me, His beautiful countenance ravaged with grief. And as He looked at me, His expression became fierce with an anger that almost became terrible with the heat of His emotion—but all at once somehow I knew that none of His hot anger was directed towards His children.

Oh yes, as He looked upon His Household, He saw many stumbling and faltering in the fierce onslaughts and He grieved terribly for us. But no, His anger burned hot against the hosts of hell and satanic princes that He saw lined up in the spiritual realm, meticulously rehearsed in their strategies and their wiles.

◆

But if the watchman sees the sword coming and does not blow the trumpet and the people are not warned, and the sword comes and takes any one of them, he is taken away in and for his perversity and iniquity, but his blood will I require at the watchman's hand. So you, son of man, I have made you a watchman for the house of Israel; therefore hear the word at My mouth and give them warning from Me. When I say, O wicked man, you shall surely die, and you do not speak to warn the wicked from his way, that wicked man shall die in his perversity and iniquity, but his blood will I require at your hand.

Ezekiel 33:6-8 The Amplified Bible

♦ THE UNLEASHING OF THE ENDTIME
SEDUCING SPIRITS ♦

And suddenly it was as though a heavy, heavenly veil was drawn back in the Spirit realm and I saw the satanic princes in their battledress standing in their chariots, directing the great mass of hellish battalions and powers and principalities—and they were standing as a great and seemingly fearsome mass in a line that stretched to eternity, waiting. And then a great shofar was sounded and the fallen satanic princes and generals took their places in front of the battalions, as the great rumbling of Satan's chariots thundered. And all as one, they bowed their heads—as the Prince of Darkness made his entrance.

And as he stood there—all terrible in his damnable arrogance and rebellion—he lifted his sword high to the heavenlies and again, as one man, I saw the princes and their battalions follow suit and I heard Lucifer's spine-chilling cry: 'It is TIME!' And the hordes of hell resounded with a great and terrible cry: 'It is TIME.' And as Lucifer turned to his fallen princes, I could hear his malicious hiss: 'IT IS TIME TO TARGET THE CHAMPIONS.'

And immediately it was as though I was back under the trees on the beautiful English lawn in front of the manor house where Jesus was standing—His countenance filled with such beauty, such grace—but His eyes seemed filled with a deep and unstoppable pain. He reached out His hand to me: 'It has begun,' He said.

I could hardly decipher His words, such was His anguish that it was as though He was choking with grief: 'My children are falling. It has begun.'

And still I could hardly make out His words for the great emotion that came from Him and the tears could not keep from falling down His cheeks as He came towards me: 'The targeting of the champions—My Father's champions here on Earth. The hosts of hell have been assigned for the past decades waiting for this hellish moment in the spirit realm, listening for the release of My endtime move from Heaven. They have heard the mighty rush of My Holy angels and so in turn they have unleashed the most violent satanic assault that Earth has yet seen since the days of My birth when Satan's wrath was unleashed through Herod against the babes in arms in a huge murderous onslaught.'

I stared at Him transfixed. And again a terrible grieving filled His countenance. 'My children, My generals, My leaders, My priests . . .'

His voice was barely audible. I could almost feel His agony, for indeed as He thought of you and I, He was suffering for us. 'The champions of My Father's Household think they are prepared. Some do not fear the enemy . . .' He hesitated. 'And that is good and right, but they also do not fear the Father. They rely on their own strength, on their own integrity, on their own valour.' He looked unwaveringly into my eyes.

'It is hard for My Father to reach these, for they are blinded by their own deceptions and will easily be overcome by the battalions you just glimpsed. For they will succumb to the snare of the great deceiver of their souls—pride. But My grieving at this moment is not for them.

'My Father loves His children.' He looked at me. 'You cannot yet understand with what tremendous passion and compassion the Father holds for His redeemed ones. They are His greatest treasures in the universe. He delights in His children. He longs for their fellowship—

for their communion with Him. The Father does not base His love for His Household on their gifting or talent or on those who in the world's eyes have so much to offer. But He has delighted to choose the foolish things of the Earth, for in His great and unfathomable wisdom He knew that those who realise that they are the most undeserving will be those who have fully embraced the fact that without His love they are completely unqualified.

'The Father knows that these are the ones who will lean their minds and hearts unquestionably on His Being— those who limp with the scars of his chastening and of their own inadequacy—those who know that within themselves there is no good thing except their hope in Him. These are His champions—and My daughter— these are the prime targets for the onslaught of the enemy that you have just seen.'

'Many of those that the Father views as His greatest generals and champions will now be assailed violently by assignments of the enemy. Each assignment is an assignment of seduction planned by Satan himself. The seducing powers and principalities have but one aim—to seduce My Household away from Me and My Father.

'I am not talking about the new believers. I am not talking about the immature or even the young men. I am talking about My leaders, My generals, My priests, those who are well versed in Me. Those who have seen terrible battles, those who have fought with Me in the dark places of the Earth, those who have led thousands upon thousands to Me across the nations, those who have built great churches, those who have brought in generational moves. I am talking about the apostles, the prophets, the pastors, the teachers, the evangelists. And I tell you, My daughter—a great and terrible coldness has been unleashed—a coldness of heart that will imbue and infect My champions' spirits. As it is written: Even the elect shall fall.

'And so brother shall rise up against brother, minister

against minister, sons against fathers, husbands against wives and the great falling away shall begin, but it shall begin in My own Household.' He was quiet. 'And it shall start with those who have been closest to us.'

A great and terrible chill went through my body. 'Jesus,' I whispered. 'How can we survive such an onslaught?'

'The major endtime assaults are divided into several camps. They are all ruthless strategies of Jezebel, the ultimate seducer and the releaser of the endtime seducing spirits. The first major seduction of My children will be in the area of morality—the lust of the flesh and the lust of the eyes, but seduction is not just confined to My children's morality. Satan's primary goal is to seduce My children away from the Father.'

'One of Satan's most lethal weapons against My ministers is another of Jezebel's strongholds—the pride of life, pride and self-righteousness. Jezebel's third great onslaught will be in the area of discouragement. This is the same weapon used against My servant Elijah and indeed many of My servants throughout the ages. Great discouragement, in turn, leading to strong delusion and finally, that of The Great Blinding.'

'The Great Blinding is a blinding of My children's hearts and of their minds which has caused them to dwell in and to live for all that which is the temporal—instead of that which is eternal.

'The world has been caught up in the great blinding to such a degree that they cannot see beyond that which they can see and touch and sense. The spirit of the world has them in its grasp and the love of the Father is not in them. I have grieved as I have watched My saints fall prey to this same spirit and as the spirit of the world has entangled them, their minds and hearts have become blinded with the deceptions of all that is temporal; and they have started to live and to desire that which brings the reward and the praise of man in the kingdom of Earth.

'But My Kingdom is not of this world, My child. And how I grieve for few there are today that truly know and understand this saying. For the ways of My Kingdom are foolish to the temporal world and so it is that in this last age many of My servants have been seduced by the spirit of the world and have suffered a great and terrible blinding. For they live more—Oh far more for what is counted and recorded in the books of man and of Earth than for that which is recorded in the books of Heaven. And that which is recorded and which counts for so much on Earth counts often for so little in My courts. For so many of My children still live for the praises and accolades and the rewards of men.

'So many of My ministers still live for that which Heaven counts as hay and as wood and what shall be burnt up in an instant as stubble when they stand before My judgement seat.

'And so I grieve with a great grieving—for My children spend their resources and the resources of My Kingdom on that which is seen and which lasts but for a moment—but eternity is built on the unseen and on the souls of men and of women. For they have been blinded with a great and terrible blinding—a blinding by the spirit of the world—but the world will perish and will pass away but he who does the will and the purposes of My Father shall live for ever.

'I have watched as some of My children have fallen morally. But My anger has been stirred as I have seen some of My ministers—those of My Own Household—turn and in their closets, pat themselves on the back and say like the Pharisees: Thank you Lord, I am not like they. I am glad I am not as they, for they are weak and surely I am strong and would never do such a thing that would make My Master ashamed. And I tell you, My child.' And He was greatly pained. 'I tell you that I have seen My children—these My ministers—sit in their homes and at their church banquets, gossiping about these fallen ones. I have seen them expose their sin, expose their nakedness and say: This is a terrible damage to the Gospel—as if in shock and as in horror—but these have **themselves** fallen victim to the pride of life. And I am grieved with a great grieving.

'For indeed pride says that it is by my own hand and by my own sufficiency that I keep the law. And self-righteousness despises the weaker and encourages itself in its own strength to keep. But I tell you that in these coming days, all that is not rooted in dependence upon Me and My Father and upon My grace, shall fall.

And even as Satan fell, so I grieve for some of My called-out ones. For they lean on their own understanding, they lean on their own integrity, then lean on their own morality, they lean on their own proficiency and they pride themselves that they are not weak like other men. *But I tell you that even as Satan fell from beholding himself as greater, so many of these, My elect, shall fall from beholding themselves instead of beholding Me.*

'And so when pride takes root in some of My servants, with it shall come a deadly self-righteousness and a critical, denigrating spirit as they compare themselves to others and they shall see the faults and the failings and the specks in their companions' and their colleagues' and their leaders' eyes and yet shall completely ignore the beam in their own. And the terrible coldness talked about in My Word shall grip their hearts and they shall not even realise that they have fallen away, for they shall be so sure of themselves and their boasting in Me.

> YOU HYPOCRITE, FIRST GET THE BEAM OF TIMBER OUT OF YOUR OWN EYE, AND THEN YOU WILL SEE CLEARLY TO TAKE THE TINY PARTICLE OUT OF YOUR BROTHER'S EYE.
>
> MATTHEW 7:5 THE AMPLIFIED BIBLE

'Tell My ministers to check their hearts, lest Satan seduce them away from their childlike trust and dependence on Me.'

'Even in the generation that preceded this present Church age, some of My greatest servants succumbed to discouragement and this led in turn to strong delusion. The enemy will do his utmost at this time to discourage and impede and roadblock My purposes and My plans. And to those whose limbs grow too weary, whose hearts grow faint with weariness, he will start to cloud their vision.' Jesus' tone was urgent.

'And visions that were birthed in power and in clarity and in the vigour of the Holy Spirit will seem to become clouded. Legions of satanic voices will be unleashed and the voice of the enemy will whisper doubt and confusion and unbelief to the weary soul. If seriously entertained, these satanic whisperings shall gain a foothold in the hearts and minds of some of My servants and they shall think to themselves: I have sowed and there is no reaping. There is no harvest. I have laboured for nought, for the fruit is so little.

'So know My child, to warn My servants that when they hear these voices, to immediately discard them, not even to entertain such a train of thought, for it is a train of thought carefully strategised by the legions of the damned with intent to discourage and to delude even the elect. For these voices will question My faithfulness. These voices will question My Word. These voices have one intent, to seduce My children away from My Father.

'When Elijah ran from Jezebel in the wilderness. He had just slain all the prophets of Baal with the sword. He had seen My mighty hand of deliverance. But on receiving Jezebel's message he ran for his life. And in these times, many of My servants who are mightily called and anointed by Me for the work in My endtime moves, have received a message from this same spirit of Jezebel that was at work against My prophet Elijah. And that message is the same today as it was then: So let the gods do to me, and more also if I make not your life as the life of one of them by tomorrow.

'And so My servants who have become weary of the battle and of standing against the darkness and warring in the high places of the Earth, have become afraid and arisen and have run for their lives and cried out to Me as Elijah did: It is enough, now Oh Lord, take away my life.'

Jesus sighed, but His sigh was not of exasperation, but filled with a deep concern and compassion.

'My Father and I have heard the cry of Our servants, My body have not understood the depth of discouragement which has gripped their souls.' He hesitated.

'I have watched from Heaven as some of My servants became weary in well-doing and because of the tremendous opposition and discouragements of the soul, they fell to discouragement, pride and eventually to strong delusions.'

I could feel the Lord's hurt. 'I have loved these men. They loved Me for many, many years with a pure heart, but they fell into Jezebel's snare and they were deceived.

'Many of My servants today face the same pitfalls. Many have served Us day by day in the hidden places of service, unseen by man but known of Me. Many of them have poured out their lives and their substance for the sake of the Gospel and for My Kingdom, but they have seen little fruit. Some have done mighty exploits, some have faithfully served day by day. But many, so many, have become weary and are ready to faint.

For Jezebel has sent her message to them saying: I will make your life as one of them (slain by the sword tomorrow.) And so the Father of Lies has sown seeds of deception in My servants' souls—questioning their faithfulness, questioning My protection—that My servants have began to doubt My very hand upon their lives. And they have become depressed and dismayed and lost their purpose that once was so clear, and like Elijah, they cry out: And I only, I am left, and the enemy seeks my life to take it away.

'Many of these ones in the past years have given themselves to activity rather than to intimate fellowship with Me. It is essential that in this season that they take time out and draw aside to Me in intimacy in My presence so that they can find refreshing.

'This assignment is far more deadly to those who are called to do as Martha, than those who sit like Mary. Many of these have great administrative gifts, they are ably equipped to do, they are equipped to run ministries, equipped to run churches, equipped to run businesses. Others have become so caught up in the activity of ministering to others that they have been caught up in the activity of serving and have lost intimacy with Me and have become depleted.

'The more intensely discouraged that My servants become, the more they have leaned on natural carnal methods to change their circumstance and have become spiritually depleted. This discouragement in turn has kept them away from My face and My presence where they would find My supernatural encouragement, strength, fortitude and divine strategy to unlock their circumstances.

'Tell them they must draw unto Me. I am their lifegiver. I am their encourager. I am their anchor. I am their sustenance. That I would allure these My children to Myself and gently as My angel spoke to Elijah say: Child, arise and eat. Draw aside and replenish yourself. Guard your minds and hearts from the father of all lies and deceiver of your souls.'

The woman was robed in purple and scarlet and bedecked with gold, precious stones, and pearls, (and she was) holding in her hand a golden cup full of the accursed offenses and the filth of her lewdness and vice. (Jer. 51:7.) And on her forehead there was inscribed a name of mystery (with a secret symbolic meaning): Babylon the great, the mother of prostitutes (idolatresses) and of the filth and atrocities and abominations of the earth. I also saw that the woman was drunk, (drunk) with the blood of the saints (God's people) and the blood of the martyrs (who witnessed) for Jesus. And when I saw her, I was utterly amazed and wondered greatly.

Revelation 17:4-6 The Amplified Bible

'This assignment is more easily discerned but far more lethal in its outward consequences, for it devours its prey. The intense seduction lures My children into the enticement of sin but eventually leaves them stripped of their ministry, calling, reputation and sometimes even their relationship with Myself and the Father and their eternal salvation.' He sighed deeply.

'The Father knows that these very ones who were drawn to Him because they knew the very weakness of their own souls—like the woman whose story I promised would be told eternally.'

I spoke. 'The woman who washed your feet?'

Jesus smiled tenderly. 'Those who have forgiven much, love much. In this last generation many came to Us from the greatest ensnarements and bondages. Once they saw Our great love for them they became Our greatest champions and bondservants, for their gratitude for receiving such a redemption, was unfathomable.

'These are the ones who have become close and tender

with Me—who would follow Me unto death.

'But if they would follow you unto death, Lord Jesus—
and they hear your voice—then how could they fall to
seducing spirits?' I asked, that chill gripping me again,
sensing the answer.

'Every weakness that these ones experienced in their
lives . . . ' His expression was so grave ' . . . every fissure,
each wound, each broken place that lies unhealed—
these satanic powers and principalities and demons shall
now target.

'Many, many of My children did not receive healing of
their minds, emotions and souls in this last generation.
And because they have lived in the Household of God for
years, many do not even realise that these scarred places
exist.

'These last days assignments have been meticulously
strategised and that is the very strength of their evil—
they have been tailor-made to each of My champions.
They know the urgent driving unmet needs of the soul:
the generational bondages of each individual called by
Me to impact this generation; the lack of nurturing; the

deep unhealed rejections and hurts of the emotions; the fatherlessness; the need for affirmation; the desire to belong; the deep isolations—all of which when not met in Me—now have laid the perfect snare for the assignments of the enemy.

'My champions shall now know a violent satanic assailing against their minds. Any thought not taken captive shall be a thought that can take violent root in their soul to lead to ensnarement. Anything from their past that has been dealt with by their own strength and not by My Spirit, shall become a snare to them and can leave them vulnerable to the enemy of their souls. Any habit not ruthlessly dealt with and put to the cross, when assigned with the searing heat of temptation, will breed and rapidly multiply.

Jesus continued. 'In this past age Jezebel has translated itself into many different forms, but one of her primary rules in this present age is her amalgamation with Babylon, the spirit of the world and lust. Lust of the flesh, lust of the eyes and the pride of life. Jezebel rules electronic media—film, television, advertising—she is the epitome of seduction in this last age. She was Delilah, Salome, Herodias. She rules pornography, adultery, lasciviousness, homosexuality, pride, power, separation, divorce and ambition and every perversion and sin of the flesh known to mankind. She tantalises, packages sin, sells it and then debases and exposes her victims before killing. Her primary targets in this last Church Age are My ministers, both men and women.'

I felt the icy chill once more. Well I knew the depth of hatred Jezebel holds for God's bondservants.

'Multitudes of My ministers today struggle with pornography. Multitudes of My ministers struggle now with lust on a daily basis. Multitudes are struggling against a terrible coldness of heart within their marriages and families.

'Many came out of a deeply sinful lifestyle or out of deep-rooted rejections and as was the way in this past generation, far too many of My children were not discipled effectively and did not receive effective healing in the areas that propelled them into that habitual sin. Also, especially among My leaders in this past generation, My Church has been so embroiled in self righteousness that if one of My children has cried for help in an area of failure, many times they have been ostracised, isolated and had their confidence betrayed. This has led to My ministers leading double lives, having a public face for their congregations whilst crying out to Me in their bedchambers because they hate what they have become. Yet they know that many will deal treacherously with them if they admit their need for help. Jezebel knows this full well and it is one of her most effective strategies. For once the champion is isolated from real help, the seducing spirits are unleashed and time after time, My child falls into adultery, fornication, homosexuality, pornography, separation and divorce. And how I and My Father grieve. For well Lucifer knows that it is often those who love us and who have hungered for Our presence who have often been the most damaged in their past— and now Satan targets the damaged places. Warn them. Warn them to guard against the great deceiver of their souls. For like Satan came to Me in the wilderness he intends to do now to those who follow Me, who lead others—to tempt—to lure—for in this most violent of testings, even My most elect shall fall.'

He hesitated and a great pain seemed to cloud His countenance. And I sensed that He was thinking about one whom I knew that He loved greatly who had been caught even that month in a prevailing sin. And I thought of the ones in this past year who had fallen in ways that were still politically acceptable to us in the Household of God—but my thoughts were not with those, but rather with those, so many of late, who had fallen morally—not acceptable—and who had lost or taken time out from their ministries.

And as I looked into Jesus' eyes, I knew that these were the ones He grieved for. For well He knew how they loved Him. In fact, some loved Him more, much more than any others. And well He knew how they must have wrestled in the still quiet hours of the early morning against sin. But because the assignments of hell had been so meticulously crafted and because Lucifer knew so well that the politics of the Church so often ensued isolation and silence in struggling with sin, one by one they had fallen to the brokenness and fissures in their own souls.

And as He looked at me, I felt that suddenly I knew how He had looked upon that rich young man. And so I prayed for all of us who had been targeted by the enemy, to be assailed in this last endtime, that even in the tumult and the fierce heat of the testings and trials and temptations, we would draw on His strength that would take us through the eye of the needle to that last lap of the narrow way that we may be counted as conquerors.

'Lord Jesus. How can we stand?' I whispered.

'There is only one way to survive the onslaught, My child.' His voice was so soft. 'Firstly. To repent of any and of all lukewarmness and backsliding in your heart and to reignite and maintain zealously your first love for Me. Secondly, to keep yourself from all idols and remain fervent in the Spirit which is the result of true fellowship in Spirit and in truth with Myself and the Father and of feeding on My Word until My Words are Spirit and Life to you,' He hesitated, 'and finally, the cross. The deception in every temptation is that which caused Adam to lead billions of souls into sin—that of selfishness. Temptation promises that which Self desires. When My children desire the promises of sin more than they desire Me— they will fall.

'The greatest weapon to survive the onslaught is for My children to take up their cross and to follow Me. To take up the cross daily and to die to everything in their souls and their mind which opposes My truth. To let go of that lower life which is the flesh and continually mortify their minds and bodies and to put to death the deeds of the flesh. My children have forgotten the power of the cross. They have thought that to die once is sufficient but the spirit of the world, with its carnality and selfishness loosed upon this present generation is so strong in these evil days—that it is only in a continual daily crucifying of their flesh that they will indeed be able to withstand temptation.

'Remember it is written, 'For you do not have a High Priest who is unable to understand and sympathise and have a shared feeling with our weaknesses and infirmities and liability to the assaults of temptation, but One who has been tempted in every respect as we are, yet without sinning.

> LET US THEN FEARLESSLY AND CONFIDENTLY AND BOLDLY DRAW NEAR TO THE THRONE OF GRACE . . . THAT WE MAY RECEIVE MERCY (FOR OUR FAILURES) AND FIND GRACE TO HELP IN GOOD TIME FOR EVERY NEED, (APPROPRIATE HELP AND WELL-TIMED HELP, COMING JUST WHEN WE NEED IT.)
> HEBREWS 4:16 THE AMPLIFIED BIBLE

'Even when you feel you are falling into the very pit of hell itself, even when it seems as if you are clinging to Me and to My Father and to My Word and its principals by a thread—when you feel that hell is sucking you in—it is then that you must cry out to Me. Cry out to My Father. Cry out Our Name, and in that very second, We will come to you and rescue you. We will draw you in and protect you from every wile of the Evil One.

'I said I will never forsake you and this is true. Even when you are in the heat of temptation—still if you cry out to Me—I will hear you.

'Speak My Word and I, the Living Word will come to your aid and accomplish that which I have promised.

'Now, warn My children. My Father's heart is grieved with a terrible grieving. Warn My beloved—that many would be saved out of the fowler's snare—that even those in the deepest mire might cry out to Me and find their way home.'

◆ SCRIPTURE REFERENCES ◆

THE FOLLOWING PAGES HAVE BEEN LEFT BLANK FOR YOU TO RECORD
PERSONAL WORDS FROM THE LORD AS YOU READ
THE JOURNAL OF THE UNKNOWN PROPHET.

NOTES

_____

_____

_____

_____

_____

_____

_____

_____

_____

_____

_____

_____

_____

_____

_____

_____

_____

_____

_____

_____

_____

_____

_____

_____

_____

_____

_____

_____

_____

_____

_____

_____

_____

_____

_____

_____

_____

_____

_____